Interactive Notebooks

LANGUAGE ARTS

Grade 5

Credits

Content Editor: Elise Craver

Visit *carsondellosa.com* for correlations to Common Core, state, national, and Canadian provincial standards.

Carson-Dellosa Publishing, LLC
PO Box 35665
Greensboro, NC 27425 USA
carsondellosa.com

978-1-4838-2472-7
02-191157784

Table of Contents

What Are Interactive Notebooks? 3

Getting Started 4

What Type of Notebook Should I Use? 5

How to Organize an Interactive Notebook . . . 6

Planning for the Year 8

Managing Interactive Notebooks
in the Classroom 10

Interactive Notebook Grading Rubric 11

Reading

Taking Interactive Notes for Reading
Comprehension 12

Making, Confirming, and
Modifying Predictions 14

Differences in Point of View 16

Reading—Literature

Determining Theme 18

Elements of Poetry 20

Reading—Informational Text

Main Ideas of a Text 22

Informational Text Structures 24

Nonfiction Text Features 26

Writing

Planning Writing 28

Using Transitional Words and Phrases . . .30

Editing and Revising 32

Finding and Evaluating Sources 34

Note Taking and Plagiarism 36

Language

Prepositions 38

Conjunctions 40

Correlative Conjunctions 42

Interjections 44

The Perfect Verb Tenses 46

Using Verb Tenses 48

Shifts in Verb Tense 50

Collective Nouns 52

Indefinite Pronouns 54

Plural Possessives 56

Punctuating Items in a Series 58

Introductory Elements in a Sentence 60

More Commas 62

Titles of Works 64

Using Context Clues 66

Prefixes, Suffixes, and Roots 68

Using Reference Materials 70

Figurative Language 72

Using Word Relationships 76

Reproducibles

Tabs 78

KWL Chart 79

Pockets 80

Shutter Folds 83

Flap Books and Flaps 85

Petal Folds 90

Accordion Folds 92

Clamshell Fold 94

Puzzle Pieces 95

Flip Book 96

© Carson-Dellosa • CD-104656

What Are Interactive Notebooks?

Interactive notebooks are a unique form of note taking. Teachers guide students through creating pages of notes on new topics. Instead of being in the traditional linear, handwritten format, notes are colorful and spread across the pages. Notes also often include drawings, diagrams, and 3-D elements to make the material understandable and relevant. Students are encouraged to complete their notebook pages in ways that make sense to them. With this personalization, no two pages are exactly the same.

Because of their creative nature, interactive notebooks allow students to be active participants in their own learning. Teachers can easily differentiate pages to address the levels and needs of each learner. The notebooks are arranged sequentially, and students can create tables of contents as they create pages, making it simple for students to use their notebooks for reference throughout the year. The interactive, easily personalized format makes interactive notebooks ideal for engaging students in learning new concepts.

Using interactive notebooks can take as much or as little time as you like. Students will initially take longer to create pages but will get faster as they become familiar with the process of creating pages. You may choose to only create a notebook page as a class at the beginning of each unit, or you may choose to create a new page for each topic within a unit. You can decide what works best for your students and schedule.

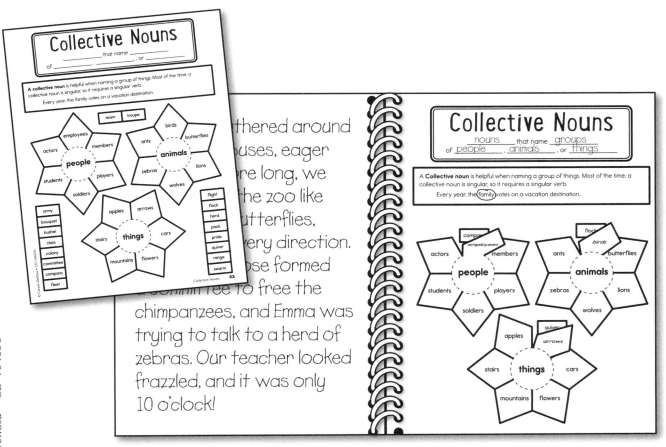

A student's interactive notebook for collective nouns

Getting Started

You can start using interactive notebooks at any point in the school year. Use the following guidelines to help you get started in your classroom. (For more specific details, management ideas, and tips, see page 10.)

1. Plan each notebook.

Use the planning template (page 9) to lay out a general plan for the topics you plan to cover in each notebook for the year.

2. Choose a notebook type.

Interactive notebooks are usually either single-subject, spiral-bound notebooks, composition books, or three-ring binders with loose-leaf paper. Each type presents pros and cons. See page 5 for a more in-depth look at each type of notebook.

3. Allow students to personalize their notebooks.

Have students decorate their notebook covers, as well as add their names and subjects. This provides a sense of ownership and emphasizes the personalized nature of the notebooks.

4. Number the pages and create the table of contents.

Have students number the bottom outside corner of each page, front and back. When completing a new page, adding a table of contents entry will be easy. Have students title the first page of each notebook "Table of Contents." Have them leave several blank pages at the front of each notebook for the table of contents. Refer to your general plan for an idea of about how many entries students will be creating.

5. Start creating pages.

Always begin a new page by adding an entry to the table of contents. Create the first notebook pages along with students to model proper format and expectations.

This book contains individual topics for you to introduce. Use the pages in the order that best fits your curriculum. You may also choose to alter the content presented to better match your school's curriculum. The provided lesson plans often do not instruct students to add color. Students should make their own choices about personalizing the content in a way that makes sense to them. Encourage students to highlight and color the pages as they desire while creating them.

After introducing topics, you may choose to add more practice pages. Use the reproducibles (pages 78–96) to easily create new notebook pages for practice or to introduce topics not addressed in this book.

Use the grading rubric (page 11) to grade students' interactive notebooks at various points throughout the year. Provide students copies of the rubric to glue into their notebooks and refer to as they create pages.

What Type of Notebook Should I Use?

Spiral Notebook

The pages in this book are formatted for a standard one-subject notebook.

Pros

- Notebook can be folded in half.
- Page size is larger.
- It is inexpensive.
- It often comes with pockets for storing materials.

Cons

- Pages can easily fall out.
- Spirals can snag or become misshapen.
- Page count and size vary widely.
- It is not as durable as a binder.

Tips

- Encase the spiral in duct tape to make it more durable.
- Keep the notebooks in a central place to prevent them from getting damaged in desks.

Composition Notebook

Pros

- Pages don't easily fall out.
- Page size and page count are standard.
- It is inexpensive.

Cons

- Notebook cannot be folded in half.
- Page size is smaller.
- It is not as durable as a binder.

Tips

- Copy pages meant for standard-sized notebooks at 85 or 90 percent. Test to see which works better for your notebook.

Binder with Loose-Leaf Paper

Pros

- Pages can be easily added, moved, or removed.
- Pages can be removed individually for grading.
- You can add full-page printed handouts.
- It has durable covers.

Cons

- Pages can easily fall out.
- Pages aren't durable.
- It is more expensive than a notebook.
- Students can easily misplace or lose pages.
- Larger size makes it more difficult to store.

Tips

- Provide hole reinforcers for damaged pages.

How to Organize an Interactive Notebook

You may organize an interactive notebook in many different ways. You may choose to organize it by unit and work sequentially through the book. Or, you may choose to create different sections that you will revisit and add to throughout the year. Choose the format that works best for your students and subject.

An interactive notebook includes different types of pages in addition to the pages students create. Non-content pages you may want to add include the following:

Title Page

This page is useful for quickly identifying notebooks. It is especially helpful in classrooms that use multiple interactive notebooks for different subjects. Have students write the subject (such as "Language Arts") on the title page of each interactive notebook. They should also include their full names. You may choose to have them include other information such as the teacher's name, classroom number, or class period.

Table of Contents

The table of contents is an integral part of the interactive notebook. It makes referencing previously created pages quick and easy for students. Make sure that students leave several pages at the beginning of each notebook for a table of contents.

Expectations and Grading Rubric

It is helpful for each student to have a copy of the expectations for creating interactive notebook pages. You may choose to include a list of expectations for parents and students to sign, as well as a grading rubric (page 11).

Unit Title Pages

Consider using a single page at the beginning of each section to separate it. Title the page with the unit name. Add a tab (page 78) to the edge of the page to make it easy to flip to the unit. Add a table of contents for only the pages in that unit.

Glossary

Reserve a six-page section at the back of the notebook where students can create a glossary. Draw a line to split in half the front and back of each page, creating 24 sections. Combine Q and R and Y and Z to fit the entire alphabet. Have students add an entry as each new vocabulary word is introduced.

Formatting Student Notebook Pages

The other major consideration for planning an interactive notebook is how to treat the left and right sides of a notebook spread. Interactive journals are usually viewed with the notebook open flat. This creates a left side and a right side. You have several options for how to treat the two sides of the spread.

Traditionally, the right side is used for the teacher-directed part of the lesson, and the left side is used for students to interact with the lesson content. The lessons in this book use this format. However, you may prefer to switch the order for your class so that the teacher-directed learning is on the left and the student input is on the right.

It can also be important to include standards, learning objectives, or essential questions in interactive notebooks. You may choose to write these on the top-left side of each page before completing the teacher-directed page on the right side. You may also choose to have students include the "Introduction" part of each lesson in that same top-left section. This is the *in, through, out* method. Students enter *in* the lesson on the top left of the page, go *through* the lesson on the right page, and exit *out* of the lesson on the bottom left with a reflection activity.

The following chart details different types of items and activities that you could include on each side.

Left Side Student Output	Right Side Teacher-Directed Learning
• learning objectives • essential questions • I Can statements • brainstorming • making connections • summarizing • making conclusions • practice problems • opinions • questions • mnemonics • drawings and diagrams	• vocabulary and definitions • mini-lessons • folding activities • steps in a process • example problems • notes • diagrams • graphic organizers • hints and tips • big ideas

Planning for the Year

Making a general plan for interactive notebooks will help with planning, grading, and testing throughout the year. You do not need to plan every single page, but knowing what topics you will cover and in what order can be helpful in many ways.

Use the Interactive Notebook Plan (page 9) to plan your units and topics and where they should be placed in the notebooks. Remember to include enough pages at the beginning for the non-content pages, such as the title page, table of contents, and grading rubric. You may also want to leave a page at the beginning of each unit to place a mini table of contents for just that section.

In addition, when planning new pages, it can be helpful to sketch the pieces you will need to create. Use the following notebook template and notes to plan new pages.

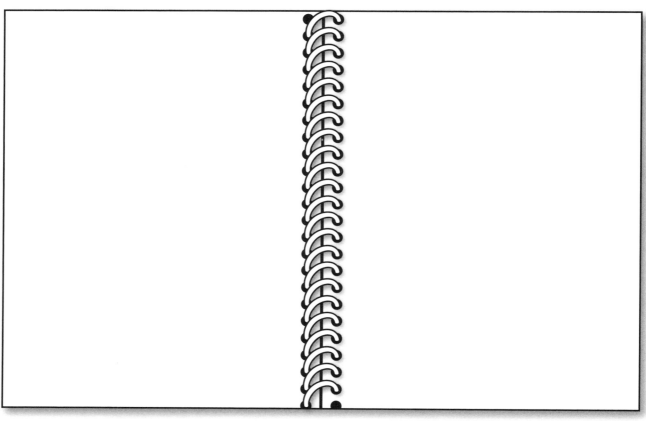

Left Side   **Right Side**

Notes

_____

_____

_____

Interactive Notebook Plan

Page	Topic	Page	Topic
1		51	
2		52	
3		53	
4		54	
5		55	
6		56	
7		57	
8		58	
9		59	
10		60	
11		61	
12		62	
13		63	
14		64	
15		65	
16		66	
17		67	
18		68	
19		69	
20		70	
21		71	
22		72	
23		73	
24		74	
25		75	
26		76	
27		77	
28		78	
29		79	
30		80	
31		81	
32		82	
33		83	
34		84	
35		85	
36		86	
37		87	
38		88	
39		89	
40		90	
41		91	
42		92	
43		93	
44		94	
45		95	
46		96	
47		97	
48		98	
49		99	
50		100	

Managing Interactive Notebooks in the Classroom

Working with Younger Students

- Use your yearly plan to preprogram a table of contents that you can copy and give to students to glue into their notebooks, instead of writing individual entries.

- Have assistants or parent volunteers precut pieces.

- Create glue sponges to make gluing easier. Place large sponges in plastic containers with white glue. The sponges will absorb the glue. Students can wipe the backs of pieces across the sponges to apply the glue with less mess.

Creating Notebook Pages

- For storing loose pieces, add a pocket to the inside back cover. Use the envelope pattern (page 81), an envelope, or a resealable plastic bag. Or, tape the bottom and side edges of the two last pages of the notebook together to create a large pocket.

- When writing under flaps, have students trace the outline of each flap so that they can visualize the writing boundary.

- Where the dashed line will be hidden on the inside of the fold, have students first fold the piece in the opposite direction so that they can see the dashed line. Then, students should fold the piece back the other way along the same fold line to create the fold in the correct direction.

- To avoid losing pieces, have students keep all of their scraps on their desks until they have finished each page.

- To contain paper scraps and avoid multiple trips to the trash can, provide small groups with small buckets or tubs.

- For students who run out of room, keep full and half sheets available. Students can glue these to the bottom of the pages and fold them up when not in use.

Dealing with Absences

- Create a model notebook for absent students to reference when they return to school.

- Have students cut a second set of pieces as they work on their own pages.

Using the Notebook

- To organize sections of the notebook, provide each student with a sheet of tabs (page 78).

- To easily find the next blank page, either cut off the top-right corner of each page as it is used or attach a long piece of yarn or ribbon to the back cover to be used as a bookmark.

Interactive Notebook Grading Rubric

4

_____ Table of contents is complete.

_____ All notebook pages are included.

_____ All notebook pages are complete.

_____ Notebook pages are neat and organized.

_____ Information is correct.

_____ Pages show personalization, evidence of learning, and original ideas.

3

_____ Table of contents is mostly complete.

_____ One notebook page is missing.

_____ Notebook pages are mostly complete.

_____ Notebook pages are mostly neat and organized.

_____ Information is mostly correct.

_____ Pages show some personalization, evidence of learning, and original ideas.

2

_____ Table of contents is missing a few entries.

_____ A few notebook pages are missing.

_____ A few notebook pages are incomplete.

_____ Notebook pages are somewhat messy and unorganized.

_____ Information has several errors.

_____ Pages show little personalization, evidence of learning, or original ideas.

1

_____ Table of contents is incomplete.

_____ Many notebook pages are missing.

_____ Many notebook pages are incomplete.

_____ Notebook pages are too messy and unorganized to use.

_____ Information is incorrect.

_____ Pages show no personalization, evidence of learning, or original ideas.

Taking Interactive Notes for Reading Comprehension

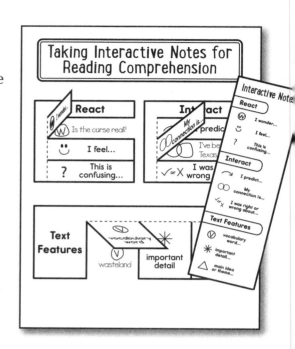

Introduction

With partners, have students make lists of things readers do before reading and after reading. Then, allow partners to share their lists with the class and compile a class list for each scenario. Create anchor charts for Before Reading and After Reading and display them around the classroom.

Creating the Notebook Page

Guide students through the following steps to complete the right-hand page in their notebooks.

1. Add a Table of Contents entry for the Taking Interactive Notes for Reading Comprehension pages.

2. Cut out the title and glue it to the top of the page.

3. Cut out the *React, Interact,* and *Text Features* pieces. Cut on the solid lines to create three flaps on each piece. Apply glue to the top and left sections of each piece. Attach the *React* and *Interact* pieces to the page below the title. Attach the *Text Features* piece to the page below the *React* and *Interact* pieces.

4. Look at each symbol and phrase. Discuss how good readers would use them during reading. Discuss how to use each symbol to begin a quick note in an interactive journal while reading. Under each flap, write an example from a current story you are reading.

5. Cut out the *Interactive Notes* bookmark. Glue it to a piece of construction paper for durability and keep it in the book you are currently reading. Use it as a reference when making notes in your interactive reading journal.

Reflect on Learning

To complete the left-hand page, have students work together to create a third anchor chart for During Reading to add to the charts completed during the lesson introduction. Each student should compile a list in his notebook of things good readers do while reading. Then, have students share their ideas and create a third anchor chart to display in the classroom.

Taking Interactive Notes for Reading Comprehension

React

(W)	I wonder...
:)	I feel...
?	This is confusing...

Interact

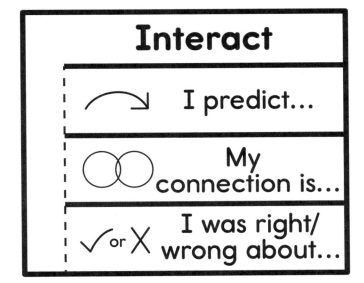

	I predict...
⊙⊙	My connection is...
✓ or ✗	I was right/ wrong about...

Text Features

(V) vocabulary word	✳ important detail	△ main idea or theme

Interactive Notes

React

- (W) I wonder...
- :) I feel...
- ?. This is confusing...

Interact
- I predict...
- ⊙⊙ My connection is...
- ✓ or ✗ I was right wrong about...

Text Features
- (V) vocabulary word...
- ✳ important detail...
- △ main idea or theme...

Making, Confirming, and Modifying Predictions

Introduction

If possible, collect the weather predictions for a few days prior to the lesson. Display the weather predictions for the next few days. As a class, discuss how reliable you think they are and why. Discuss how they are based on information from satellites, radar, and meteorological patterns. Then, display the weather predictions from the past few days. Discuss if they were all correct and why or why not. Tell students that making predictions while reading is like making weather predictions, because readers are constantly gathering new information and changing their predictions (which may still turn out to be incorrect).

Creating the Notebook Page

Guide students through the following steps to complete the right-hand page in their notebooks.

1. Add a Table of Contents entry for the Making, Confirming, and Modifying Predictions pages.

2. Cut out the title and glue it to the top of the page.

3. Cut out the *A prediction is* piece and glue it below the title.

4. Complete the text. (A prediction is an educated **guess** about what will happen in a **text**. Making predictions should happen **before**, **during**, and **after** reading.)

5. Cut out all of the pieces and arrows. Arrange them on the page to create a flow chart. The *Start Here* piece should be at the top with an arrow pointing to the *Do you have* piece below it. Place two arrows pointing down from that piece with a *yes* or *no* piece on top of each. Finally, place the *Keep your prediction* and *Revise your prediction* pieces in a row at the bottom. Place the return arrows on the left and right sides of the flow chart to connect the bottom pieces to the top piece. Glue all of the pieces to the page.

6. Start at the top of the flow chart when making predictions. Discuss how the flow chart works and how readers should always be learning new information and confirming or revising their predictions based on that information. Even when a text is finished, a reader may predict what happens next for a character.

Reflect on Learning

To complete the left-hand page, have students follow the flow chart and make and revise predictions for a short text they are currently reading or a short story from a basal textbook.

Making, Confirming, and Modifying Predictions

A **prediction** is an educated _____ about what will happen in a text. Making predictions should happen _____, _____, and _____ reading.

Start Here

Make a prediction and start reading.

Do you have any information that confirms your prediction?

Keep your prediction and continue reading.

Revise your prediction and continue reading.

yes

no

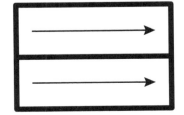

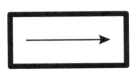

Differences in Point of View

Introduction

Write these two sentences on the board: *As the flakes slowly piled up outside the window, the _____ could barely contain his excitement. "More snow means more shoveling, more slush, and more traffic," moaned the _____ .* Have students suggest nouns to fill in the blanks. As a class, discuss how they decided on the best noun for each blank and how the point of view affected each narrator's view of the same event (a snowy day).

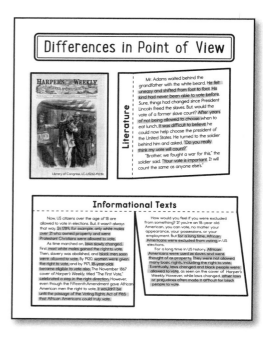

Creating the Notebook Page

Guide students through the following steps to complete the right-hand page in their notebooks.

1. Add a Table of Contents entry for the Differences in Point of View pages.

2. Cut out the title and glue it to the top of the page.

3. Cut out the image and glue it to the top left of the page.

4. Cut out the *Literature* flap. Apply glue to the back of the left section and attach it to the right of the image.

5. Cut out the *Informational Texts* flap book. Cut on the solid line to create two flaps. Apply glue to the back of the top section. Attach it to the bottom of the page.

6. Look at the image and discuss the event it shows. Then, read each piece of text. Discuss how each piece of text discusses the same event from a different point of view. Under each flap, write how the point of view affects the text. In addition, for the informational texts, add notes to compare and contrast how the points of view affect the different accounts of the same topic.

7. On each flap, underline or highlight key words and phrases that show the author's point of view.

Reflect on Learning

To complete the left-hand page, have each student write a short paragraph from the point of view of a common inanimate object such as a pencil or chair.

Determining Theme

Theme is the **BIG** idea of a text.

You can determine the theme of a text by asking and answering questions about the story elements.

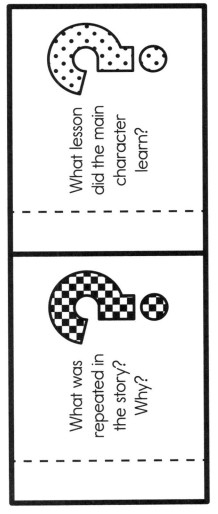

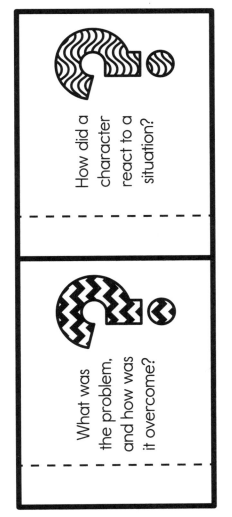

How did the main character change?

What lesson did the main character learn?

How did a character react to a situation?

How did this story make me feel? Why?

What was repeated in the story? Why?

What was the problem, and how was it overcome?

Elements of Poetry

Introduction

Display several different poems. Have students discuss with partners the similarities and differences they see between the poems. Then, as a class, compare and contrast the poems.

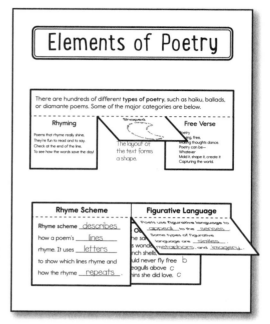

Creating the Notebook Page

Guide students through the following steps to complete the right-hand page in their notebooks.

1. Add a Table of Contents entry for the Elements of Poetry pages.

2. Cut out the title and glue it to the top of the page.

3. Cut out the *Rhyming, Shaped, Free Verse* flap book. Cut on the solid lines to create three flaps. Apply glue to the back of the top section and attach it to the page below the title.

4. Read the flap book and discuss each type of poetry. Identify how each example poem demonstrates the poetry type. Under the flap, write a short description to explain how that type of poetry is different from the other types.

5. Cut out the *Rhyme Scheme, Figurative Language* flap book. Cut on the solid line to create two flaps. Apply glue to the back of the top section and attach it to the page below the poetry types flap book.

6. Cut out the poem. Glue it under the *Rhyme Scheme, Figurative Language* flap book.

7. Complete the definitions for *rhyme scheme* and *figurative language*. (Rhyme scheme **describes** how a poem's **lines** rhyme. It uses **letters** to show which lines rhyme and how the rhyme **repeats**. Poets use figurative language to **appeal** to the **senses**. Some types of figurative language are **similes**, **metaphors**, and **imagery**.)

8. On the poem under the flaps, write the rhyme scheme at the end of the lines of the poem. Highlight or underline the figurative language used in the poem.

Reflect on Learning

To complete the left-hand page, display a poem. Or, provide students with copies to glue in their notebooks. Have students identify the type of poem, the rhyme scheme, and any figurative language used in the poem.

Elements of Poetry

There are hundreds of different **types of poetry**, such as haiku, ballads, or diamante poems. Some of the major categories are below.

Rhyming

Poems that rhyme really shine,
They're fun to read and to say.
Check at the end of the line,
To see how the words save the day!

Shaped

Free Verse

Poetry
Flowing, free,
Making thoughts dance.
Poetry can be—
Whatever
Mold it, shape it, create it
Capturing the world.

Rhyme Scheme

Rhyme scheme _____

how a poem's _____

rhyme. It uses _____

to show which lines rhyme and

how the rhyme _____ .

Figurative Language

Poets use **figurative language** to

_____ to the _____ .

Some types of figurative

language are _____ ,

_____ , and _____ .

By the Ocean

As she walked along the sandy shore
with delight as nature's wonders she did see
starfish, whitecaps, conch shells, and more.
She knew that she would never fly free
like the tissue-paper seagulls above
or swim with the dolphins she did love.

Main Ideas of a Text

Introduction

Review main idea. Have students work in small groups. Assign each group a short story or informational text. Each group should find the main idea of their text. Allow each group to share the main idea of their text and the supporting details that support the main idea.

Creating the Notebook Page

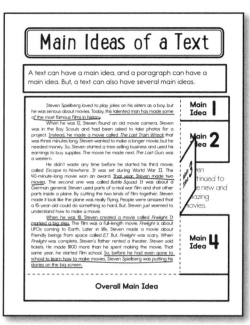

Guide students through the following steps to complete the right-hand page in their notebooks.

1. Add a Table of Contents entry for the Main Ideas of a Text pages.

2. Cut out the title and glue it to the top of the page.

3. Cut out the *A text can have* piece and glue it below the title.

4. Discuss how a text can have more than one main idea. Authors can make multiple points in a text to support their main idea. Each paragraph can have a main idea, which in turn supports the main idea of the entire passage.

5. Cut out the passage piece. Cut on the solid lines to create four flaps on the right side and a long flap on the bottom. Apply glue to the back of the passage and attach it to the page. Be careful not to apply glue to the bottom flap.

6. Read the passage. Under each flap to the right, write the main idea of each paragraph. Under the bottom flap, write the main idea of the entire passage. Underline or highlight supporting details in the passage as you read.

Reflect on Learning

To complete the left-hand page, have students reflect on why an author would have more than one main idea. They may wish to refer to the passage on the right-hand page to support their reflections.

Main Ideas of a Text

A text can have a main idea, and a paragraph can have a main idea. But, a text can also have several main ideas.

Steven Spielberg loved to play jokes on his sisters as a boy, but he was serious about movies. Today, this talented man has made some of the most famous films in history.

When he was 12, Steven found an old movie camera. Steven was in the Boy Scouts and had been asked to take photos for a project. Instead, he made a movie called *The Last Train Wreck* that was three minutes long. Steven wanted to make a longer movie, but he needed money. So, Steven started a tree-selling business and used his earnings to buy supplies. The movie he made next, *The Last Gun*, was a western.

He didn't waste any time before he started his third movie, called *Escape to Nowhere*. It was set during World War II. The 40-minute-long movie won an award. That year, Steven made two movies. The second one was called *Battle Squad*. It was about a German general. Steven used parts of a real war film and shot other parts inside a plane. By cutting the two kinds of film together, Steven made it look like the plane was really flying. People were amazed that a 15-year-old could do something so hard. But, Steven just seemed to understand how to make a movie.

When he was 18, Steven created a movie called *Firelight*. It marked a big step. The film was a full-length movie. *Firelight* is about UFOs coming to Earth. Later in life, Steven made a movie about friendly beings from space called *E.T.* But, *Firelight* was scary. When *Firelight* was complete, Steven's father rented a theater. Steven sold tickets. He made $100 more than he spent making the movie. That same year, he started film school. So, before he had even gone to school to learn how to make movies, Steven Spielberg was putting his stories on the big screen.

Main Idea 1

Main Idea 2

Main Idea 3

Main Idea 4

Overall Main Idea

Informational Text Structures

Have students describe what type of article or text would be most helpful in each of the following situations: trying to decide between two different cell phones, learning about a tree frog, fixing a flat bicycle tire, learning what causes a drought, and making a craft. Discuss if the same type of text could be used for more than one situation and why or why not.

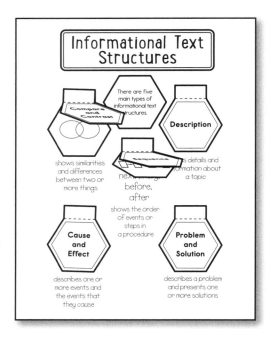

Creating the Notebook Page

Guide students through the following steps to complete the right-hand page in their notebooks.

1. Add a Table of Contents entry for the Informational Text Structures pages.

2. Cut out the title and glue it to the top of the page.

3. Cut out the *There are five main types* piece and glue it below the title.

4. Cut out all of the flaps.

5. Match each informational text structure to the diagram that best describes it. Apply glue to the gray glue section on the diagram flap and place the informational text structure flap on top to create a two-flap book. Apply glue to the back of the top section and attach it to the page. Leave space for writing below each flap book.

6. Under each flap, write signal words that help you identify that text structure. Below the flap, write characteristics that are unique to that text structure. Discuss how it is useful for readers to be able to identify a text's structure, because specific text structures are useful to audiences for different purposes.

Reflect on Learning

To complete the left-hand page, have students identify and compare the text structures in two different texts. Students should record key words and characteristics that helped identify the text structure in each text.

Informational Text Structures

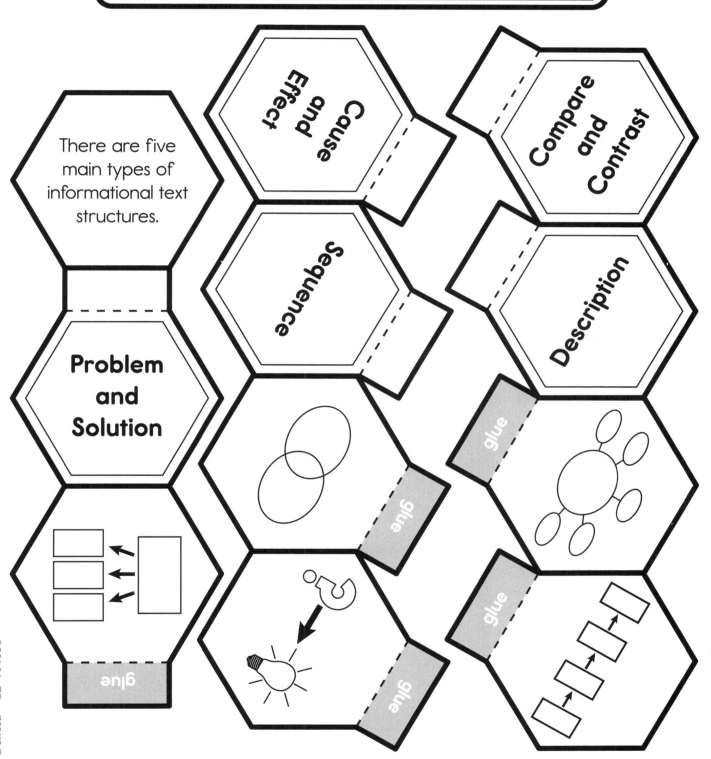

There are five main types of informational text structures.

Cause and Effect

Compare and Contrast

Sequence

Description

Problem and Solution

glue

glue

glue

glue

glue

Nonfiction Text Features

Introduction

Before the lesson, print a copy of an old newspaper article that shows a dense block of text and a modern article with headings, subheadings, and other text features. Display the two articles. As a class, discuss the differences between the articles. Ask students to describe which text makes it easier to find information and why.

Creating the Notebook Page

Guide students through the following steps to complete the right-hand page in their notebooks.

1. Add a Table of Contents entry for the Nonfiction Text Features pages.

2. Cut out the title and glue it to the top of the page.

3. Cut out the magazine page flap. Apply glue to the back of the left section and attach it to the page.

4. Read the article.

5. On the flap, identify the nonfiction text features such as bold and italic text, headings, subheadings, sidebars, photographs, maps, illustrations, captions, etc. Label each text feature.

6. Under the flap, write at least three questions about the article. Beside each question, write the answer and the text feature(s) that could be used to easily find the answer in the article.

Reflect on Learning

To complete the left-hand page, have students work with partners. Students should ask their partners three of their questions about the article on the right-hand page. Partners should write the answers in their notebooks and write the text features they used to answer each question. Then, students should compare answers to see if their partners used the same text features to find the answers to their questions.

Gold Rush!

Did you know that the North American gold rushes were responsible for things such as the rapid increase of the population of the American West and the name of the San Francisco 49ers?

In the Beginning

Gold rushes are not uncommon. In 1829, gold was discovered on land belonging to the Cherokee tribe. Eager **prospectors**, as people searching for gold were known as, flooded northern Georgia. The small tourist town of Dahlonega (dah-LAHN-eh-gah) still exists today. *Dahlonega* is Cherokee for "yellow money."

Western Gold Rushes

An 1848 gold rush sent 250,000 people west, hoping to strike it rich. The large amount of fortune-seekers that flooded west in 1849 became known as "forty-niners." By 1850, California's population was so high it became an official state. Some miners did become wealthy, but most didn't make enough money to even return home. San Francisco and Sacramento grew out of this gold rush. A decade later, when gold was found at Colorado's Pike's Peak, it was Denver's turn to flourish.

In 1874, gold in South Dakota's Black Hills sent prospectors swarming into Sioux Indian territory. In 1897, prospectors headed north, braving the bitter Alaskan cold in search of gold.

Panning for Gold

To pan for gold, prospectors choose a wide, shallow metal pan. They fill it with sand and swirl it in water. The heavy gold pieces sink; fine gold powder sticks to the edges.

Fun Facts

- The first US gold rush occurred in North Carolina 50 years before gold was found in Georgia.

- Other gold rushes occurred in Canada, Australia, and South Africa.

- The largest gold nugget found in Australia weighed more than 200 pounds (75 kg).

Library of Congress, LC-USZ62-7120
Three prospectors, Spriggs, Lamb, and Dillon, are panning for gold in 1889.

Planning Writing

Introduction

Review author's purpose. Tell students that the three main reasons authors write are to persuade, to inform, or to entertain. Within each category are even more reasons to write. Give students a hand signal for each category. A thumbs-up stands for *p*, or *persuade*. A fist with the pinkie finger sticking out stands for *i*, or *inform*, and a fist stands for *e*, or *entertain*. Then, list different types of writing one at a time such as poem, letter to the editor, article, advertisement, or fable. Students should respond to each by making the appropriate signs with their hands. Tell students that as authors, they have to make several decisions before they start writing, including why they are writing.

Creating the Notebook Page

Guide students through the following steps to complete the right-hand page in their notebooks.

1. Add a Table of Contents entry for the Planning Writing pages.

2. Cut out the title and glue it to the top of the page.

3. Cut out the *Before starting* flap book. Cut on the solid lines to create four flaps. Apply glue to the back of the center section and attach it to the page below the title.

4. Under each flap, give more information and examples. For example, under the *What format* flap, you may choose to write different types of formats.

5. Cut out the *Graphic Organizers* flap book. Cut on the solid lines to create four flaps. Apply glue to the back of the top section and attach it to the bottom of the page.

6. On the top of each flap, draw an example of the graphic organizer. Under each flap, write the types of writing it works best for. For example, a sequence graphic organizer is helpful for a set of instructions or a story with a beginning, middle, and end, but not for a descriptive article.

Reflect on Learning

To complete the left-hand page, have students begin planning a piece of writing. Students should answer all four questions from the right-hand side of the page and use a graphic organizer to begin outlining their pieces.

Planning Writing

Why am I writing?

What format best fits my purpose?

Before starting a writing piece, ask and answer these questions.

What is my **main idea**?

Who am I writing for?

Graphic Organizers for Planning My Writing

Web	Sequence	Outline	Venn Diagram

Using Transitional Words and Phrases

Before the lesson, find a set of step-by-step instructions or a paragraph with transitional words and phrases. Cover the transitional words and phrases. Display the text without the transition words. Have students read it and discuss how easy or difficult it was to read and understand. Then, uncover the transitional words and phrases. Discuss how the transitional words and phrases affect understanding.

Creating the Notebook Page

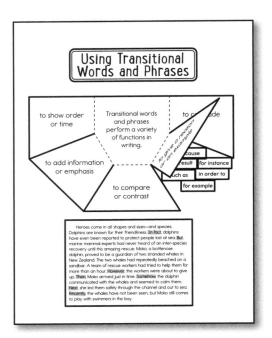

Guide students through the following steps to complete the right-hand page in their notebooks.

1. Add a Table of Contents entry for the Using Transitional Words and Phrases pages.

2. Cut out the title and glue it to the top of the page.

3. Cut out the *Transitional words* flap book. Cut on the solid lines to create five flaps. Apply glue to the back of the center section and attach it to the page below the title.

4. Discuss what transitional words and phrases are and how they can serve different purposes in a text.

5. Cut out the transitional words and phrases. Glue each transitional word or phrase under the correct flap, depending on the purpose it serves in a text. Discuss how some transitional words and phrases may serve more than one purpose. Add any additional transitional words and phrases, such as *but, then, next,* etc., to the underside of each flap.

6. Cut out the passage and glue it to the bottom of the page.

7. Read the passage. Circle or highlight the transitional words and phrases.

Reflect on Learning

To complete the left-hand page, have each student write a short, silly paragraph about a day when she woke up and was levitating. Students should use at least five transitional words or phrases and should underline each one.

Answer Key
Circled: In fact; But; However; Then; Somehow; Next; Recently

Using Transitional Words and Phrases

also	additionally
always	as a result
because	before

Transitional words and phrases perform a variety of functions in writing.

- to show order or time
- to conclude
- to add information or emphasis
- to give a reason or an example
- to compare or contrast

compared to	definitely	during
especially	except	finally

however	in fact
for instance	in contrast
for example	in conclusion
following	in addition

such as	while
similarly	too
like	to sum up
in order to	therefore

Heroes come in all shapes and sizes—and species. Dolphins are known for their friendliness. In fact, dolphins have even been reported to protect people lost at sea. But, marine mammal experts had never heard of an inter-species recovery until this amazing rescue. Moko, a bottlenose dolphin, proved to be a guardian of two stranded whales in New Zealand. The two whales had repeatedly beached on a sandbar. A team of rescue workers had tried to help them for more than an hour. However, the workers were about to give up. Then, Moko arrived just in time. Somehow, the dolphin communicated with the whales and seemed to calm them. Next, she led them safely through the channel and out to sea. Recently, the whales have not been seen, but Moko still comes to play with swimmers in the bay.

Editing and Revising

Introduction

Display an unedited and unrevised piece of writing and an edited and revised piece of writing. Have students read each piece. As a class, discuss each piece. Which piece feels more finished? Which author seems more trustworthy? Why? Discuss how editing and revising writing is an important step in the writing process.

Creating the Notebook Page

Guide students through the following steps to complete the right-hand page in their notebooks.

1. Add a Table of Contents entry for the Editing and Revising pages.

2. Cut out the title and glue it to the top of the page.

3. Cut out the *editing vs. revising* piece. Cut on the solid lines to create two flaps. Apply glue to the back of the top and middle sections and attach the piece below the title.

4. Under each flap, write a short description of each term to highlight the differences between editing and revising. Editing generally refers to correcting mechanics such as capitalization, spelling, punctuation, and grammar. Revising is improving writing by adding or removing details or words, reorganizing content, and making things easier for the reader to understand.

5. Cut out the editing and revising checklists. Glue them to the left side of the page.

6. Discuss the types of things you should look for in each stage of fixes.

7. Cut out the writing piece and glue it to the right of the checklists.

8. Use the checklists to help you correct the writing piece.

Reflect on Learning

To complete the left-hand page, display the unedited piece from the lesson introduction or provide copies for students to glue in their notebooks. Then, have students use the editing and revising checklists to show how they would improve the writing piece.

Editing and Revising

Both editing and revising are used to improve writing. But, how are they different?

editing

vs.

revising

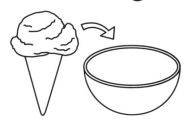

Editing Checklist

- [ ] All words are properly capitalized.
- [ ] Each sentence ends with the correct ending punctuation.
- [ ] Commas are placed where they belong.
- [ ] Quotation marks show where speech starts and ends.
- [ ] All of the words are spelled correctly.
- [ ] The subjects and verbs match.
- [ ] The sentences are complete and not run-ons.

Revising Checklist

- [ ] The writing has a beginning, a middle, and an end.
- [ ] The writing is focused and stays on topic.
- [ ] The writing is well organized.
- [ ] The sentences are easy for readers to understand.
- [ ] The writing includes enough details and support.
- [ ] The writing uses a variety of words.
- [ ] The writing uses exciting verbs and interesting adjectives.
- [ ] The introduction and conclusion are satisfying.

Sometimes, citys grow across state or provincial boundary. For example, part of flin Flon (a canadian mining city is in Saskatchewan the other part is in manitoba. Most persons in the city live on the Manitoba side Another Canadian city, lloydminster, lays in both alberta and Saskatchewan. In the United states, the Kansas City metropolitan area (which includes the separate cities of Kansas city, Kansas and Kansas City, Missouri straddles state boundaries Other state spanning urban areas include the following Texarkana, Florala and Lake Tahoe.

Finding and Evaluating Sources

Introduction

Before the lesson, find a sales flyer for a local store. Choose an item in the sales flyer. Tell students that you heard from a friend's cousin that he could get a good deal on the item. Then, display the sales flyer. Ask students which "sale" they trust more and why. Discuss what makes sources trustworthy. Tell students that when doing research, they should also evaluate whether their sources are trustworthy and reliable before using the information.

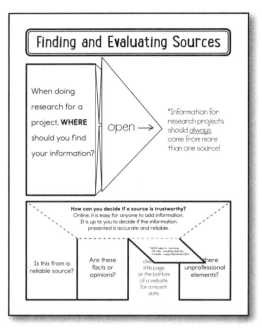

Creating the Notebook Page

Guide students through the following steps to complete the right-hand page in their notebooks.

1. Add a Table of Contents entry for the Finding and Evaluating Sources pages.

2. Cut out the title and glue it to the top of the page.

3. Cut out the *When doing research* clamshell piece. Fold and unfold on the dashed lines, folding toward the inside. Pull the top and bottom of the vertical dashed line together. Then, keeping the top and bottom together, bring the right-hand side of the paper to the left. It should meet the thin black line. Flatten the clamshell. Apply glue to the back of the folded piece and glue it below the title.

4. Open the clamshell and write sources, such as *encyclopedias, web sites, brochures, articles, experiences*, etc., on the inside of the clamshell. Close the clamshell. Discuss how important it is to get information for a research project from multiple sources. On the notebook page to the right of the clamshell piece, make a note about the importance of gathering information from more than one source.

5. Cut out the flap book. Cut on the solid lines to create four flaps. Apply glue to the back of the top section and attach it to the bottom of the page.

6. Read the flap book and discuss what makes a source trustworthy. Under each flap, give examples and more details. For example, under the *unprofessional elements* flap, give examples such as spelling and grammar errors and silly clip art.

Reflect on Learning

To complete the left-hand page, display three to five different sources. Have students judge each source as trustworthy or untrustworthy and give reasons for each judgment.

Finding and Evaluating Sources

When doing research for a project, **WHERE** should you find your information?

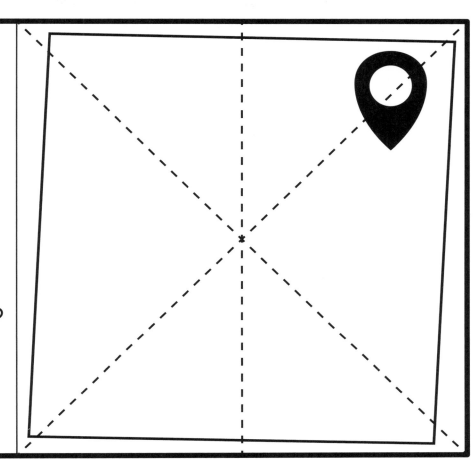

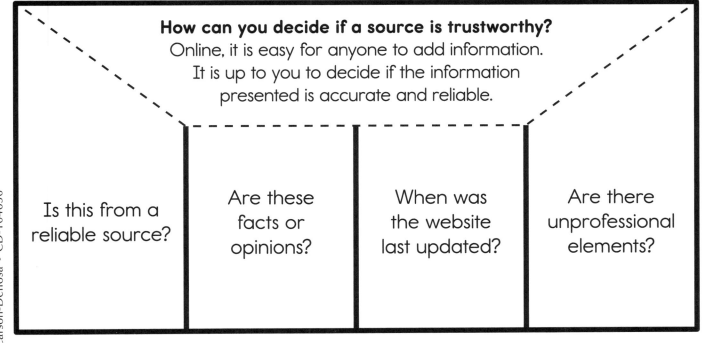

How can you decide if a source is trustworthy?
Online, it is easy for anyone to add information. It is up to you to decide if the information presented is accurate and reliable.

Is this from a reliable source?

Are these facts or opinions?

When was the website last updated?

Are there unprofessional elements?

Note Taking and Plagiarism

As a class, discuss stealing. Is taking someone's laptop wrong? Why or why not? How about taking someone's lunch? What about putting your name on someone's poem and saying you wrote it? What if you take a piece of someone's writing and put it in your research paper as a supporting detail? Discuss how it can get confusing when you start using other people's work to support your ideas, but stress that using other people's work without giving them credit is always plagiarism.

Creating the Notebook Page

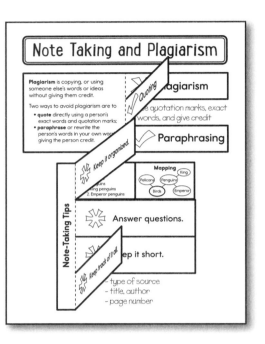

Guide students through the following steps to complete the right-hand page in their notebooks.

1. Add a Table of Contents entry for the Note Taking and Plagiarism pages.

2. Cut out the title and glue it to the top of the page.

3. Cut out the *Plagiarism is* flap book. Cut on the solid lines to create three flaps. Apply glue to the back of the left side and attach it to the page below the title.

4. Discuss what plagiarism is and isn't. Under each flap, write what the term means in your own words and how it can be used when doing research and writing reports.

5. Cut out the *Note-Taking Tips* flap book. Cut on the solid lines to create four flaps. Apply glue to the back of the left side and attach it to the bottom of the page.

6. Cut out the *Outlines* and *Mapping* pieces. Glue them under the *Keep it organized* flap.

7. Under the other flaps, write short explanations and tips for note taking. For example, under the *Keep it short* flap, give examples for how to take short notes. Under the *Keep track of it all* flap, give examples for how to cite your sources.

Reflect on Learning

To complete the left-hand page, display a short text. Or, provide students with copies to glue in their notebooks. Have students use the text to practice taking notes.

Note Taking and Plagiarism

Plagiarism is copying, or using someone else's words or ideas without giving them credit.

Two ways to avoid plagiarism are to

- **quote** directly using a person's exact words and quotation marks;
- **paraphrase** or rewrite the person's words in your own words, giving the person credit.

 Plagiarism

 Quoting

 Paraphrasing

Note-Taking Tips

Keep it organized.

Answer questions.

Keep it short.

Keep track of it all.

Outlines

I. Birds
A. Pelicans
B. Penguins
  1. King penguins
  2. Emperor penguins

Mapping

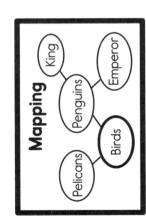

Prepositions

Introduction

Have each student get a textbook and a pencil. Say positional prepositions such as *around, below, above, in,* etc., and have students act out the prepositions with the pencils and textbooks. Repeat several times. Discuss how prepositions are useful to describe positions, as well as to give more information.

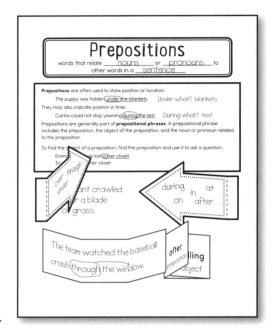

Creating the Notebook Page

Guide students through the following steps to complete the right-hand page in their notebooks.

1. Add a Table of Contents entry for the Prepositions pages.

2. Cut out the title and glue it to the top of the page.

3. Complete the definition of *prepositions* (words that relate **nouns** or **pronouns** to other words in a **sentence**).

4. Cut out the *Prepositions are* piece and glue it below the title.

5. Discuss what prepositions are and the different ways they can be used. Look at the example sentences and identify the preposition in each sentence. Discuss prepositional phrases and how to identify the object in a prepositional phrase. Draw arrows to identify the objects in all of the example sentences. Underline the prepositional phrases in the example sentences.

6. Cut out the arrow flaps. Apply glue to the back of the narrow sections and glue them below the *Prepositions are* piece.

7. On each arrow, write examples of prepositions. You may choose to write positional prepositions on one arrow and time prepositions on the other arrow. Under each flap, write an example sentence using one preposition.

8. Cut out the rectangles. Fold on the dashed lines so that the gray glue sections are on the back of the flap books. Apply glue to the gray glue sections and attach them to the bottom of the page.

9. Label the words on the flaps *preposition* or *object*. Open the flaps and write a sentence using the given preposition and object. Underline the prepositional phrase, circle the preposition, and draw an arrow from the preposition to the object.

Reflect on Learning

To complete the left-hand page, have each student choose any book from her desk and open it to a random page. Students should identify and record at least five prepositional phrases. Have students circle the prepositions and draw arrows to the objects in the phrases.

Prepositions

words that relate _____ or _____ to

other words in a _____

Prepositions are often used to show position or location.

    The puppy was hidden under the blankets.

They may also indicate position in time.

    Carlos could not stop yawning during the test.

Prepositions are generally part of **prepositional phrases**. A prepositional phrase includes the preposition, the object of the preposition, and the noun or pronoun related to the preposition.

To find the object of a preposition, find the preposition and use it to ask a question.

    Emma's shoe was lost in her closet.

    In where?   In her closet

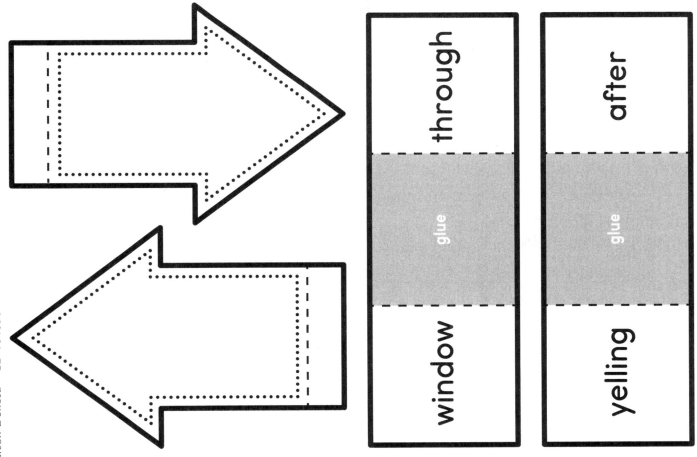

through

glue

window

after

glue

yelling

Conjunctions

Introduction

Review clauses. Display several simple sentences. Have students identify the subjects and verbs in each. Then, display several clauses such as *dogs howl, as the dogs howl,* and *dogs howl when.* Have students identify the subject and verb in each clause. Discuss which clauses are incomplete thoughts, and why.

Creating the Notebook Page

Guide students through the following steps to complete the right-hand page in their notebooks.

1. Add a Table of Contents entry for the Conjunctions pages.

2. Cut out the title and glue it to the top of the page.

3. Complete the definition of *conjunctions* (words that join **words** or groups of words called **clauses**).

4. Cut out the *Coordinating Conjunctions, Subordinating Conjunctions* piece. Cut on the solid line to create two flaps. Apply glue to the back of the left side and attach the piece below the title.

5. Discuss each type of conjunction. Identify the conjunctions and clauses in the example sentences. Under each flap, write examples of each type of conjunction, such as *and, but, or, nor, so,* and *after, though, unless, when, where, since,* and *as.*

6. Cut out the flap book. Cut on the solid lines to create six flaps. Apply glue to the back of the center section and attach it to the bottom of the page.

7. Read each sentence. Circle the conjunction. Under the flap, write the type of conjunction used.

Reflect on Learning

To complete the left-hand page, have students write two sentences using coordinating conjunctions and two sentences using subordinating conjunctions. Students should circle the conjunctions and underline the clauses in their sentences.

Conjunctions

words that join _____ or groups
of words called _____

Coordinating conjunctions combine related sentences or independent clauses.

I visited Japan, and I tried to eat sushi wrapped in seaweed there.

Coordinating Conjunctions

Subordinating conjunctions begin dependent clauses, which cannot stand alone as sentences.

Since some seaweed is not edible, you can't use all seaweed in sushi.

Subordinating Conjunctions

If you look at London's Big Ben clock tower, you will have an idea of how tall some giant redwood trees are.

Sometimes, small clusters of berries will grow on the tops of potato plants, and they look like little green cherry tomatoes.

Because a popcorn kernel's shell is waterproof, steam is trapped inside until the kernel explodes.

Identify the conjunction and conjunction type.

Vibration is a back-and-forth movement, and it produces light, heat, and sound.

The quagga, an extinct mammal related to the zebra, was striped only on the front, but was solid brown on its hindquarters.

Although a tarantula's bite is painful, the venom is weaker than the venom of a typical bee.

Correlative Conjunctions

Introduction

Review conjunctions. Write coordinating and subordinating conjunctions on index cards. Give each student a conjunction index card and a blank index card. Have each student write a clause on the blank index card. Each student should then use his conjunction and clause to write a silly sentence. Then, have students switch conjunctions and repeat. Allow students to share their silly sentences.

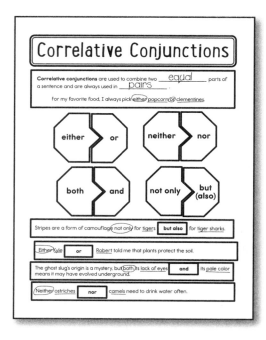

Creating the Notebook Page

Guide students through the following steps to complete the right-hand page in their notebooks.

1. Add a Table of Contents entry for the Correlative Conjunctions pages.

2. Cut out the title and glue it to the top of the page.

3. Cut out the *Correlative conjunctions are* piece and glue it below the title.

4. Complete the definition of *correlative conjunctions*. (Correlative conjunctions are used to combine two **equal** parts of a sentence and are always used in **pairs**.) Circle the correlative conjunctions in the example sentence and underline the equal parts of the sentence they combine.

5. Cut out the half-octagon puzzle pieces. Match the correlative conjunction pairs. Glue the pairs to the page.

6. Cut out the sentences and glue them to the bottom of the page. Cut out the correlative conjunction pieces.

7. Read each sentence. Circle the first correlative conjunction used. Glue the matching correlative conjunction in the space. Underline the equal parts of the sentence they combine.

Reflect on Learning

To complete the left-hand page, have students write sentences using each pair of correlative conjunctions.

Correlative Conjunctions

Correlative conjunctions are used to combine two _____ parts of a sentence and are always used in _____ .

For my favorite food, I always pick either popcorn or clementines.

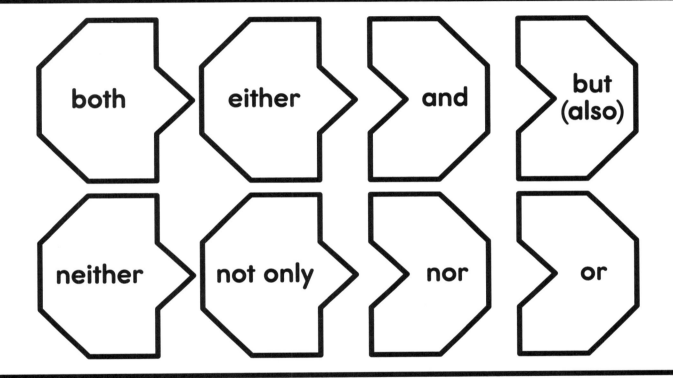

both   either   and   but (also)

neither   not only   nor   or

Stripes are a form of camouflage not only for tigers   for tiger sharks.

Either Kyle   Robert told me that plants protect the soil.

The ghost slug's origin is a mystery, but both its lack of eyes   its pale color means it may have evolved underground.

Neither ostriches   camels need to drink water often.

| and | but also | nor | or |

Interjections

Introduction

Ask students to discuss with partners how they can add emotion to their writing. Then, allow partners to share their ideas with the class. Record their ideas on the board. Then, ask students to discuss with their partners how they can add emotion to dialogue. Repeat the first activity. Tell students that interjections can be helpful when adding emotion to writing and dialogue.

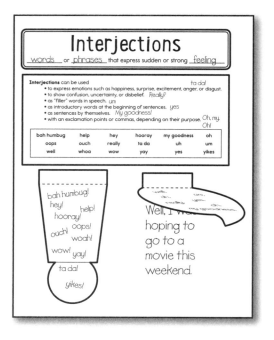

Creating the Notebook Page

Guide students through the following steps to complete the right-hand page in their notebooks.

1. Add a Table of Contents entry for the Interjections pages.

2. Cut out the title and glue it to the top of the page.

3. Complete the definition of *interjections* (**words** or **phrases** that express sudden or strong **feeling**).

4. Cut out the *Interjections can be used* piece and glue it below the title.

5. Discuss what interjections are and how they can be used. Look at the list of interjections and choose one word to illustrate each example.

6. Cut out the exclamation point and comma flaps. Apply glue to the back of the top sections and attach them to the bottom of the page.

7. On the exclamation point, add interjections from the word bank that would be followed by an exclamation point. Add any others you can think of. Under the flap, write an example sentence or two using an interjection from the flap.

8. Repeat step 7 with the comma flap.

Reflect on Learning

To complete the left-hand page, have each student write a short dialogue about a surprise. Students should use and circle at least four interjections.

Interjections

_____ or _____ that express sudden or strong _____

Interjections can be used
- to express emotions such as happiness, surprise, excitement, anger, or disgust.
- to show confusion, uncertainty, or disbelief.
- as "filler" words in speech.
- as introductory words at the beginning of sentences.
- as sentences by themselves.
- with an exclamation points or commas, depending on their purpose.

bah humbug	help	hey	hooray	my goodness	oh
oops	ouch	really	ta-da	uh	um
well	whoa	wow	yay	yes	yikes

The Perfect Verb Tenses

Introduction

Review verb tenses. Write a sentence in the present tense, such as *Davis walks his dog*, on the board. Have students rewrite the sentence in the past, future, present progressive, past progressive, and future progressive tenses.

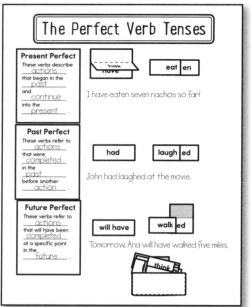

Creating the Notebook Page

Guide students through the following steps to complete the right-hand page in their notebooks.

1. Add a Table of Contents entry for the The Perfect Verb Tenses pages.

2. Cut out the title and glue it to the top of the page.

3. Cut out the *Present Perfect*, *Past Perfect*, and *Future Perfect* pieces. Glue them along the left side of the page.

4. Cut out the pocket. Apply glue to the back of the tabs and attach the pocket to the bottom-right side of the page.

5. Complete the definition of *present perfect* (these verbs describe **actions** that began in the **past** and **continue** into the **present**), *past perfect* (these verbs refer to **actions** that were **completed** in the **past** before another **action**), and *future perfect* (these verbs refer to **actions** that will have been **completed** at a specific point in the **future**).

6. Cut out the *has* and *have* flaps, an *en* piece, and the 14 verb pieces. Apply glue to the gray glue section and stack the flaps to create a single two-flap book. Glue it to the right of the *Present Perfect* piece. Leave a space wide enough for a verb card and then glue the *en* piece to the right.

7. Place a verb card in the space between the flaps and the *en* piece to create a verb phrase such as *has eaten* or *have driven*. You may need to fold cards or write irregular forms on the back of each verb card. Choose a verb phrase and use it to write a complete sentence below the pieces. Store the verb cards in the pocket created in step 4.

8. Repeat steps 6 and 7 with past perfect and future perfect verbs. Use the *had* and *ed* pieces for past perfect. Use the *will have* piece and the *ed* and *en* flaps for future perfect.

Reflect on Learning

To complete the left-hand page, write several sentences in simple past and simple future tense on the board. Have students rewrite each sentence in a perfect tense and identify in which perfect tense it is written.

The Perfect Verb Tenses

Present Perfect

These verbs describe _____ that began in the _____ and _____ into the _____.

Past Perfect

These verbs refer to _____ that were _____ in the _____ before another _____.

Future Perfect

These verbs refer to _____ that will have been _____ at a specific point in the _____.

	glue
has	have

had	will have

en
ed

ed

glue
en

eat	think
give	walk
write	help
throw	sing
type	laugh
draw	speak
text	drive

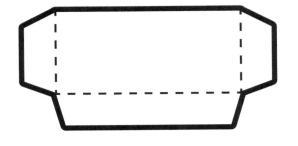

Using Verb Tenses

Introduction

Review subjects, verbs, and objects. Write several simple sentences, such as *Becca sent a text to her friend* and *Kade is drinking all of the lemonade,* on the board. Have students identify the subject, verb, and object in each sentence.

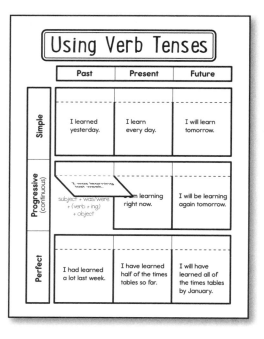

Creating the Notebook Page

Guide students through the following steps to complete the right-hand page in their notebooks.

1. Add a Table of Contents entry for the Using Verb Tenses pages.

2. Cut out the title and glue it to the top of the page.

3. Cut out the *Past, Present, Future* label and glue it below the title.

4. Cut out the *Simple, Progressive, Perfect* label and glue it along the left-hand side of the page.

5. Cut out the sentence flap books. Cut on the solid lines to create three flaps on each flap book. Apply glue to the back of each top section and attach it to the correct place in the grid.

6. Read each example sentence. Discuss when it would be appropriate to use each verb tense in writing. Identify the subject, verb, and object in each sentence. You may choose to color each part of the sentence a different color. Under the flap, write the "sentence math" for each tense. For example, simple future tense would be *subject + will verb + object* and present progressive tense would be *subject + am/is (verb + ing) + object.*

Reflect on Learning

To complete the left-hand page, have students choose an action, such as *riding a horse* or *eating popcorn,* and use it to complete a similar chart that shows an example sentence for each of the nine verb tenses.

Using Verb Tenses

	Past	Present	Future
Simple	I learned yesterday.	I learn every day.	I will learn tomorrow.
Progressive (continuous)	I was learning last week.	I am learning right now.	I will be learning again tomorrow.
Perfect	I had learned a lot last week.	I have learned half of the times tables so far.	I will have learned all of the times tables by January.

Shifts in Verb Tense

Review verb tenses. Before the lesson, glue copies of or write sentences with different tenses on index cards. Make enough cards for each student to have one card. Give each student one card. Have students read their sentences. Challenge students to decide on the tense of their sentences and find other students with sentences of the same tense. Collect the cards, shuffle them, and repeat the activity.

Creating the Notebook Page

Guide students through the following steps to complete the right-hand page in their notebooks.

1. Add a Table of Contents entry for the Shifts in Verb Tense pages.

2. Cut out the title and glue it to the top of the page.

3. Cut out the *When the verb tense* piece and glue it below the title.

4. Discuss what a shift in verb tense is and why writers should avoid changes in verb tense.

5. Cut out the flap book. Cut on the solid lines to create six flaps. Apply glue to the back of the center section and attach it to the page.

6. Read each sentence. Identify the shift in verb tense and circle the incorrect verb. Write the corrected sentence under the flap.

Reflect on Learning

To complete the left-hand page, display a piece of writing with shifts in verb tense. Or, provide copies that students can glue in their notebooks. Have students count, record, and correct the incorrect shifts in verb tense.

Answer Key

A biodegradable water bottle is made from corn and **disappears** in about 80 days. Jackrabbits have excellent hearing in part because they **have** long, funnel-shaped ears. Mosquitoes are more attracted to people who **wear** dark clothing than people who wear light colors. On May 10, 1869, the transcontinental railroad was completed, and bells **rang** in cities across the country. Modern safety pins were patented in 1849, although they **were** used in the Bronze Age. Most Americans did not use forks until the 1850s because spoons **were** more commonplace.

Shifts in Verb Tense

When the verb tense in a sentence, paragraph, or piece of writing changes, it can confuse the reader because the time may have changed between past, present, and future. Unless characters are traveling through time, keep an eye out for changing verb tenses!

A biodegradable water bottle is made from corn and disappeared in about 80 days.

On May 10, 1869, the transcontinental railroad was completed, and bells ring in cities across the country.

Correct the shifts in verb tense.

Jackrabbits have excellent hearing in part because they had long, funnel-shaped ears.

Modern safety pins were patented in 1849, although they are used in the Bronze Age.

Mosquitoes are more attracted to people who wore dark clothing than people who wear light colors.

Most Americans did not use forks until the 1850s because spoons are more commonplace.

Collective Nouns

Introduction

Review nouns and subject-verb agreement. Pair students and challenge each pair to think of one singular and one plural example of each noun type (person, place, thing, and abstract). Possible plural abstract nouns include *truths, liberties, fears,* etc. Then, have students think of eight verbs. Finally, have partners randomly pair the nouns and verbs to create eight silly sentences. They should be careful to make sure their subjects and verbs agree. Allow students to share their sentences.

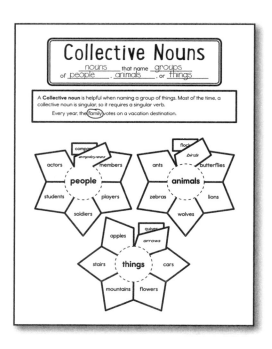

Creating the Notebook Page

Guide students through the following steps to complete the right-hand page in their notebooks.

1. Add a Table of Contents entry for the Collective Nouns pages.

2. Cut out the title and glue it to the top of the page.

3. Complete the definition of *collective nouns* (**nouns** that name **groups** of **people**, **animals**, or **things**).

4. Cut out the *Collective nouns are* piece and glue it below the title.

5. Discuss what collective nouns are and how they should be treated in a sentence. Read the example sentence and identify the collective noun and verb. Discuss the subject-verb agreement.

6. Cut out the flowers. Cut on the solid lines to create six flaps on each flower. Apply glue to the back of the center section of each flower and attach the flowers to the page.

7. Cut out the collective noun labels. Read each label. Match each to a plural noun on the correct flower and glue it under the flap. Discuss how some collective nouns may match more than one plural noun. Find the best match for each. Use a dictionary if needed.

Reflect on Learning

To complete the left-hand page, have students use at least four of the collective nouns from the right-hand page to write a paragraph about a silly day at school. Students should be careful to use the correct subject-verb agreement with the collective nouns.

Answer Key
People: actors, troupe; employees, company; members, committee; players, team; soldiers, army; students, class
Animals: ants, colony; birds, flock; butterflies, swarm; lions, pride; wolves, pack; zebras, herd
Things: apples, bushel; arrows, quiver; cars, fleet; flowers, bouquet; mountains, range; stairs, flight

Collective Nouns

_____ that name _____
of _____ , _____ , or _____

A **collective noun** is helpful when naming a group of things. Most of the time, a collective noun is singular, so it requires a singular verb.

Every year, the family votes on a vacation destination.

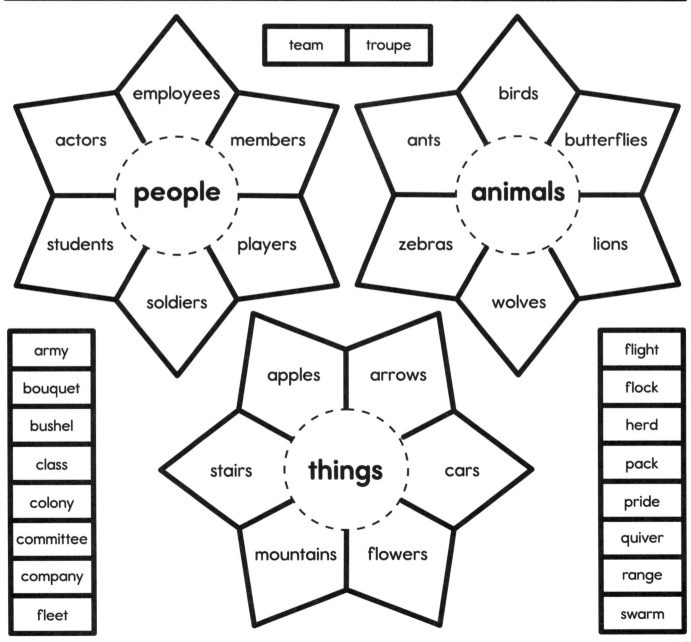

| team | troupe |

people — employees, actors, members, students, players, soldiers

animals — birds, ants, butterflies, zebras, lions, wolves

things — apples, arrows, stairs, cars, mountains, flowers

| army |
| bouquet |
| bushel |
| class |
| colony |
| committee |
| company |
| fleet |

| flight |
| flock |
| herd |
| pack |
| pride |
| quiver |
| range |
| swarm |

Indefinite Pronouns

Introduction

Review pronouns. Display several simple sentences, such as *Victor and Zoe watched the puppies*, *Tia told a joke*, and *Mom bought new pencils for my brother and me*, on the board. Have students identify the nouns that can be replaced by pronouns and replace them. Repeat with several different sentences.

Creating the Notebook Page

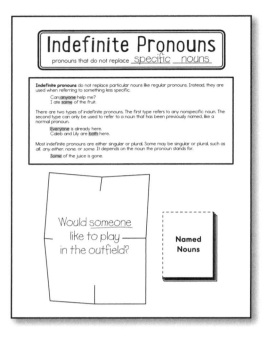

Guide students through the following steps to complete the right-hand page in their notebooks.

1. Add a Table of Contents entry for the Indefinite Pronouns pages.

2. Cut out the title and glue it to the top of the page.

3. Complete the definition of *indefinite pronouns* (pronouns that do not replace **specific nouns**).

4. Cut out the *Indefinite pronouns do not* piece and glue it below the title.

5. Discuss how indefinite pronouns are similar to and different from regular pronouns. Read each example sentence and identify the indefinite pronoun.

6. Cut out the two rectangles. Place one rectangle facedown. Fold it in half on the horizontal fold line. Then, fold it in half on the remaining fold line so that it forms a small book with the gray glue section on the back and the title on the front. Apply glue to the gray glue section and attach it to the bottom left of the page. Repeat with the remaining rectangle.

7. Read the example pronouns in each book. Then, open each book fully and write an example sentence inside.

Reflect on Learning

To complete the left-hand page, have students choose at least four different indefinite pronouns and use each one in a complete sentence.

54

Indefinite Pronouns

pronouns that do not replace _____ _____

Indefinite pronouns do not replace particular nouns like regular pronouns do. Instead, they are used when referring to something less specific.

> Can anyone help me?
> I ate some of the fruit.

There are two types of indefinite pronouns. The first type refers to any nonspecific noun. The second type can only be used to refer to a noun that has been previously named, like a normal pronoun.

> Everyone is already here.
> Caleb and Lily are both here.

Most indefinite pronouns are either singular or plural. Some may be singular or plural, such as *all, any, either, none,* or *some.* It depends on the noun the pronoun stands for.

> Some of the juice is gone.

someone nothing nobody everything everybody anyone	something somebody none no one everyone anything anybody	several one many either both another	some neither few each any all
glue	**Nonspecific Nouns**	glue	**Named Nouns**

Plural Possessives

Introduction

Review the difference between plural nouns and possessive nouns. Write pairs of words on index cards. For example, write *kittens* and *kitten's* on separate index cards. On the board, write sentences for the words, leaving blanks where the words belong, such as *The _____ played with the yarn* and *The _____ yarn was all over the floor.* Challenge students to place the correct index card in the correct blank. As a class, discuss how students knew which card belonged in which blank. Then, have students think about how they would show the plural form of the possessive noun (*kittens*) in the second sentence.

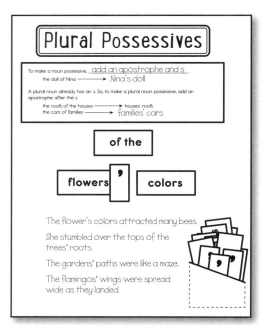

Creating the Notebook Page

Guide students through the following steps to complete the right-hand page in their notebooks.

1. Add a Table of Contents entry for the Plural Possessives pages.

2. Cut out the title and glue it to the top of the page.

3. Cut out the *To make a noun* piece and glue it under the title.

4. Discuss possessive nouns and the difference between singular possessive nouns and plural possessive nouns. Complete the sentence (To make a noun possessive, **add an apostrophe and s**). Complete each example.

5. Cut out the pocket. Fold the rectangle in on the dashed line. Apply glue to the back of the tabs and fold them in to close the pocket. Apply glue to the back of the pocket and attach it to the bottom right of the page.

6. Cut out the word pieces and the apostrophe pieces.

7. Use the words to form phrases such as *paths of the gardens, wings of the flamingos, colors of the wings*, etc. Then, move the cards and add the apostrophes to form possessive plural phrases such as *gardens' paths, flamingos' wings, wings' colors*, etc. Finally, use each phrase to write a sentence on the page. Store the words and apostrophes in the pocket.

Reflect on Learning

To complete the left-hand page, have each student write a short reflection about how plural possessives are different than singular possessives and why they are treated differently than singular possessives in writing.

56

Plural Possessives

To make a noun possessive, _____ .

      the doll of Nina ————————→

A plural noun already has an *s*. So, to make a plural noun possessive, add an apostrophe after the *s*.

      the roofs of the houses ————————→ houses' roofs

      the cars of families ————————→

flowers	colors	roots
bees		
airplanes	paths	flights
trees		
flamingos		
gardens	leaves	wings
zoos		

, , , ,

of the

of the

Punctuating Items in a Series

Introduction

Write this sentence on the board: *I would like to invite my parents, my teacher and the principal.* Have students identify the list of items in the sentence. Discuss if the list is punctuated correctly and how it affects the reader's interpretation of the sentence. (It can lead the reader to think that the teacher and the principal are the speaker's parents.) Explain that including a comma before the last item in a list can help avoid confusion.

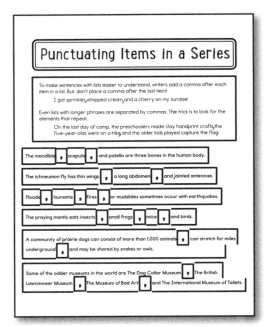

Creating the Notebook Page

Guide students through the following steps to complete the right-hand page in their notebooks.

1. Add a Table of Contents entry for the Punctuating Items in a Series pages.

2. Cut out the title and glue it to the top of the page.

3. Cut out the *To make sentences* piece and glue it below the title.

4. Discuss why and where commas should be added in lists. Read the example sentences and add commas in the correct places. Discuss how to find the correct places when lists include longer phrases instead of single items.

5. Cut out the sentences. Cut out the strip of commas. To avoid losing the small comma pieces, keep the commas together as a strip and cut off each comma as you use it.

6. Working with one sentence at a time, read the sentence. Identify the items in a list. Cut apart the sentence between each item. Glue the sentence on the page and glue a comma between each item in the list. Sentence strips may need to be cut into multiple pieces.

7. Repeat step 6 with each sentence. Two extra commas are provided in case any are lost.

Reflect on Learning

To complete the left-hand page, have students decide the best way to punctuate a sentence that includes a list within a list. On the board, write the sentence *To keep busy, Ava read a few books organized her clothes jewelry and makeup and helped her mom bake cookies.* Students should copy the sentence and add commas where needed.

58

Introductory Elements in a Sentence

Many different types of phrases can be used to introduce the main clause of a sentence. Most introductory elements should be followed by commas.

Meanwhile, Sasha worked on her high jump.
To avoid getting sick, Quan avoided the rest of his family.
As the clock struck three, the students bolted from their seats.
Panting and gasping for air, Trey crossed the finish line.
The loudest cat of all, Bandit let everyone know he was hungry.

| To dodge the snowball | Samira started walking down the boardwalk. |

| Jumping up in alarm | Xander dove into a nearby snowbank and returned fire. |

| Banging on the xylophone | the baby added to the noise in an already zany house. |

| Singing an off-key tune | Mr. Murphy ran for the car, muttering about being late. |

More Commas

Introduction

Before the lesson, find a short passage and remove the commas. Then, make copies. Give each student a copy of the passage. Have students add the missing commas to the passage. As a class, review and discuss the missing commas.

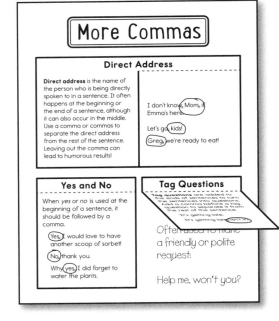

Creating the Notebook Page

Guide students through the following steps to complete the right-hand page in their notebooks.

1. Add a Table of Contents entry for the More Commas pages.

2. Cut out the title and glue it to the top of the page.

3. Cut out the *Direct Address* piece. Cut on the solid line to create a flap. Apply glue to the back of the left side and top section and attach it below the title.

4. Discuss what direct address is and how commas must be used to set it off. Read each example sentence. Identify why it shows direct address and how the comma is used in each example. Under the flap, write more information such as how to use direct address in the middle of a sentence. Give another example sentence.

5. Cut out the *Yes and No* and *Tag Questions* flaps. Apply glue to the back of the top sections and attach them to the bottom of the page.

6. Repeat step 4 with the *Yes and No* and *Tag Questions* flaps.

Reflect on Learning

To complete the left-hand page, have students write example sentences for the three types of comma use.

More Commas

Direct Address

Direct address is the name of the person who is being directly spoken to in a sentence. It often happens at the beginning or the end of a sentence, although it can also occur in the middle. Use a comma or commas to separate the direct address from the rest of the sentence. Leaving out the comma can lead to humorous results!

I don't know, Mom, if Emma's here.

Let's go, kids!

Greg, we're ready to eat!

Yes and No

When *yes* or *no* is used at the beginning of a sentence, it should be followed by a comma.

Yes, I would love to have another scoop of sorbet!

No, thank you.

Why yes, I did forget to water the plants.

Tag Questions

Tag questions are added to the ends of sentences to turn the sentences into questions. Add a comma before a tag question to separate it from the rest of the sentence.

It's getting late.

It's getting late, isn't it?

Titles of Works

Introduction

Give each student an index card. Have each student write the name of her favorite movie, favorite book, and favorite song. Explain that titles of movies, books, and songs are proper nouns like all other names and should be capitalized properly. Have students work with partners to check that their titles are capitalized properly. Explain that when used in writing, titles should also be treated differently to let readers know that they are titles.

Creating the Notebook Page

Guide students through the following steps to complete the right-hand page in their notebooks.

1. Add a Table of Contents entry for the Titles of Works pages.

2. Cut out the title and glue it to the top of the page.

3. Cut out the movie poster and glue it below the title.

4. Discuss how depending on the type of work the title is for (for example, movie, novel, or poem) and if the writer is handwriting or typing, titles will either use italics, quotation marks, or underlining. Explain that works will either need italics or quotation marks and that underlining is only used when writing by hand because people cannot easily write in italics.

5. Cut out the flap book. Cut on the solid lines to create three flaps. Apply glue to the back of the top section and attach it to the bottom of the page.

6. Cut out the labels. Sort and glue them under the first or second flaps. Under the *underlining* flap, describe when underlining should be used.

7. Around the movie poster, write examples of titles that are correctly capitalized and underlined or in quotation marks.

Reflect on Learning

To complete the left-hand page, have students use the titles they wrote in the lesson introduction in complete sentences. Students should write each title properly capitalized and underlined or in quotation marks.

Answer Key
Italics: books, magazines, movies, newspapers, plays, TV shows
Quotation Marks: articles, chapter titles, essays, poems, short stories, song titles

Titles of Works

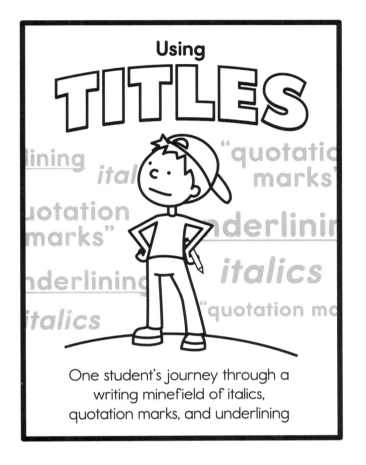

Using

TITLES

One student's journey through a writing minefield of italics, quotation marks, and underlining

articles
books
chapter titles
essays
magazines
movies
newspapers
plays
poems
short stories
song titles
TV shows

When should you use...

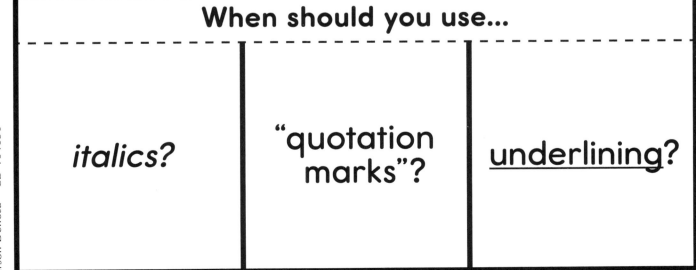

italics?	"quotation marks"?	<u>underlining</u>?

Using Context Clues

Introduction

Display a short passage with several unfamiliar words. As a class, read through the text. Stop at each unfamiliar word and look it up in the dictionary. After reading the text, discuss how stopping to look up every unfamiliar word in the dictionary affected students' understanding and enjoyment of the passage. Explain that good readers often use other strategies such as using context clues and rereading to understand unfamiliar words, because those strategies don't interrupt the flow of a text.

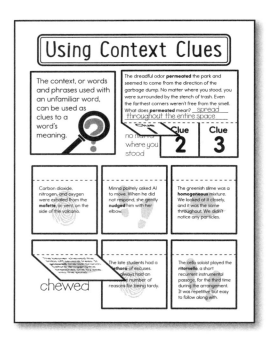

Creating the Notebook Page

Guide students through the following steps to complete the right-hand page in their notebooks.

1. Add a Table of Contents entry for the Using Context Clues pages.

2. Cut out the title and glue it to the top of the page.

3. Cut out the magnifying glass piece and glue it to the left side of the page below the title.

4. Discuss what *context* and *context clues* are and how they might be found immediately beside words, or earlier or later in a paragraph or passage.

5. Cut out the passage and clues piece. Cut on the solid lines to create three flaps. Apply glue to the back of the top section and attach it to the right of the magnifying glass piece.

6. Read the passage. Answer the question. Under each flap, write a clue that helped you answer the question.

7. Cut out the six flaps. Apply glue to the back of the top sections and attach them to the bottom of the page.

8. Read each sentence. Use context clues to determine the meaning of each bold word and write the meaning under the flap.

Reflect on Learning

To complete the left-hand page, return to the passage from the introduction. Have each student choose an unfamiliar word from the text, define it, and provide the context clues they used to determine their definition.

Using Context Clues

The context, or words and phrases used with an unfamiliar word, can be used as clues to a word's meaning.

The dreadful odor **permeated** the park and seemed to come from the direction of the garbage dump. No matter where you stood, you were surrounded by the stench of trash. Even the farthest corners weren't free from the smell. What does **permeated** mean? _____

_____

| Clue 1 | Clue 2 | Clue 3 |

Carbon dioxide, nitrogen, and oxygen were exhaled from the **mofette**, or vent, on the side of the volcano.

Minna politely asked Al to move. When he did not respond, she gently **nudged** him with her elbow.

The greenish slime was a **homogeneous** mixture. We looked at it closely, and it was the same throughout. We didn't notice any particles.

The beaver chewed the limbs off several trees. It **gnawed** one last branch before dragging the branches one by one into the pond.

The late students had a **plethora** of excuses. They always had an excessive number of reasons for being tardy.

The cello soloist played the **ritornello**, a short recurrent instrumental passage, for the third time during the arrangement. It was repetitive but easy to follow along with.

Prefixes, Suffixes, and Roots

This lesson is designed to allow students to choose four words to focus on. Or, make two copies of the right-hand page and have students work on all eight words across two notebook pages.

Introduction

Review simple prefixes and suffixes. As a class, brainstorm a list of common prefixes and suffixes such as *re-*, *mis-*, *un-*, *-ed*, *-ing*, and *-ion*. Write the prefixes and suffixes on the board. Beginning with the word *do*, have the first student choose any prefix or suffix to add to the word to create a new word. The next student should change one word part to create a new word. For example, if the first student says *redo*, the next student may choose *rewind*. Then, the next student may change *rewind* to *winding*. Continue until all students have contributed words.

Creating the Notebook Page

Guide students through the following steps to complete the right-hand page in their notebooks.

1. Add a Table of Contents entry for the Prefixes, Suffixes, and Roots pages.

2. Cut out the title and glue it to the top of the page.

3. Cut out the four square pieces. Fold and unfold each piece to the inside on the three dashed lines. Place one piece so that the fold lines form an X with a horizontal line through it. Pull the left and right sides together until they touch. Keeping the sides touching, bring the top edge down to meet the bottom edge and press to flatten, creating a triangle that unfolds into a square. Repeat with the other three squares. Apply glue to the back of each triangle and attach it to the page, leaving enough room under each to write sentences.

4. Choose and cut out four word pieces. Glue one word in the box at the top of each square.

5. Use the word to complete the parts of each square. Write the prefix, root, and suffix of the word. (Not all words will have both a prefix and a suffix.) Then, define the word, and write a synonym and antonym for the word. Discuss the similarities among words that share similar roots, prefixes, and suffixes.

6. In the space under each triangle, write a sentence using the word.

Reflect on Learning

To complete the left-hand page, have each student choose a new word that shares a root or affix with a word on the right-hand page. Each student should write the prefix, root, suffix, definition, and a synonym and antonym for the word. Then, he should describe how it is related to the similar word(s) on the right-hand side of the page.

Prefixes, Suffixes, and Roots

disruptive	distraction	eruption	inspection
interrupt	spectator	speculate	subtract

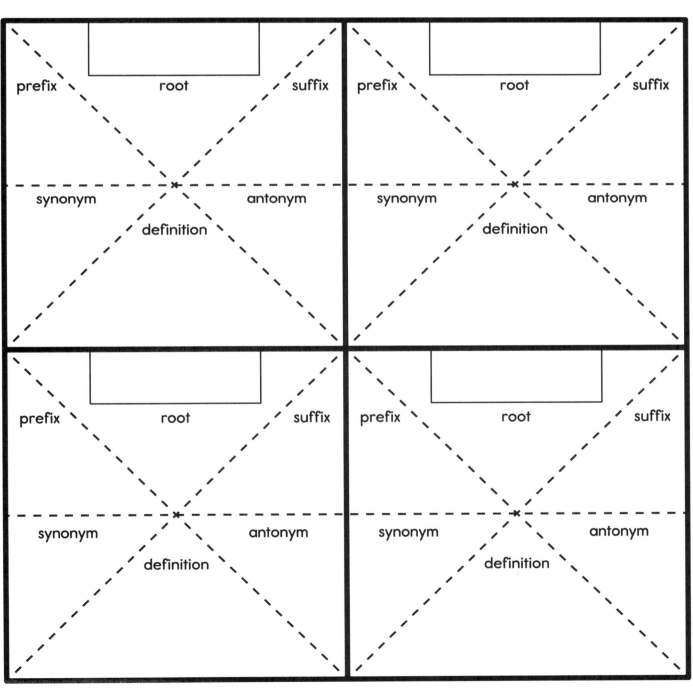

Using Reference Materials

Introduction

Before the lesson, gather several different versions of dictionaries, glossaries, and thesauruses, including printouts of entries from online versions. Divide students into three groups and give each group the dictionaries, glossaries, or thesauruses. Have each group compare and contrast the different versions of their reference materials and develop a list of general characteristics. Allow groups to share their lists.

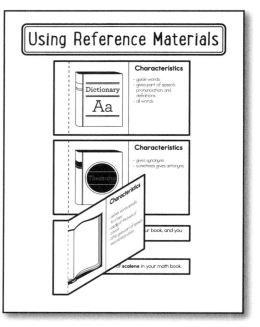

Creating the Notebook Page

Guide students through the following steps to complete the right-hand page in their notebooks.

1. Add a Table of Contents entry for the Using Reference Materials pages.

2. Cut out the title and glue it to the top of the page.

3. Cut out the *Dictionary, Thesaurus,* and *Glossary* pieces. Apply glue to the back of the narrow left sections and attach them to the page.

4. Discuss the differences between each reference material. Record the defining characteristics for each reference material under *Characteristics*.

5. Cut out the situation pieces.

6. Read each situation. Decide which reference material would be most useful and glue the situation under that flap.

Reflect on Learning

To complete the left-hand page, have students reflect on the pros and cons of using print versus online reference materials.

Using Reference Materials

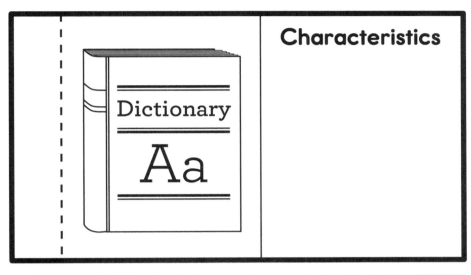

Characteristics

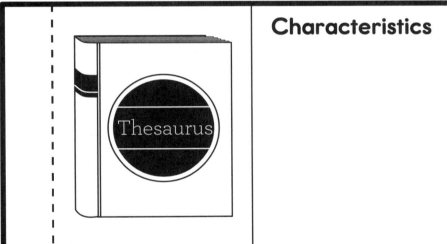

Characteristics

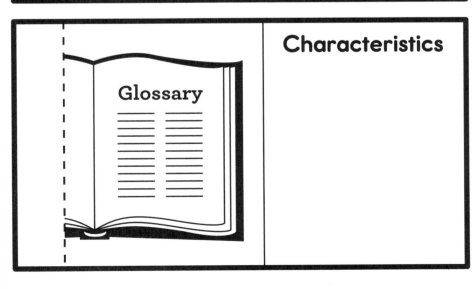

Characteristics

Genealogy is in bold print in your book, and you want to know what it means.

Find the definitions of your spelling words: **breezy, eldest, grateful,** and **stackable.**

Locate an antonym for the word **similarly** to use in your compare and contrast paper.

Find the part of speech of **context.**

Locate the pronunciation of **scrivener** or **scudo.**

Find a different word for **excellent** because you have used it six times in your paper.

Find more than 15 synonyms for **run.**

Find the definition of **scalene** in your math book.

Figurative Language

The pieces for this lesson are found on pages 73–75. This lesson is designed to introduce one or more literary devices at a time and can be taught during a period of days or weeks. If desired, place each literary device on a separate page.

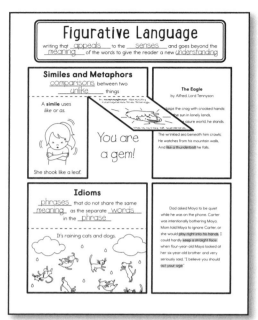

Introduction

Display several sentences using figurative language, such as *We must have walked a thousand miles* and *The bad grade yelled in Jon's backpack.* Discuss the difference between literal and nonliteral language in each sentence by having students identify what actually did and did not happen. Then, discuss why writers would want to include things that did not actually happen.

Creating the Notebook Page

Guide students through the following steps to complete the right-hand page in their notebooks.

1. Add a Table of Contents entry for the Figurative Language pages.

2. Cut out the title and glue it to the top of the page.

3. Complete the definition of *figurative language* (writing that **appeals** to the **senses** and goes beyond the **meaning** of the words to give the reader a new **understanding**).

4. Cut out the teaching pieces. If the piece has flaps, cut on the solid line to create two flaps. Apply glue to the back of the top sections and attach them to the left side of the page.

5. Complete the definition of *similes and metaphors* (**comparisons** between two **unlike** things), *idioms* (**phrases** that do not share the same **meaning** as the separate **words** in the **phrase**), *personification* (giving **human** characteristics to **things**, **animals**, or **ideas**), *hyperbole* (an **exaggeration** to emphasize a **point**), *alliteration* (**repeating** the first **consonant** sound in several words), or *onomatopoeia* (the use of words that **sound** like their **meanings**). Read the example for each. Write a new example under each flap.

6. Cut out the example pieces and glue them to the right of the correct teaching pieces.

7. Read the example text and identify examples of the literary device.

Reflect on Learning

To complete the left-hand page, have students write example sentences using each type of figurative language. Then, have students write short reflections on how they can use figurative language to enhance their writing.

Figurative Language

writing that _____ to the _____ and goes beyond the _____ of the words to give the reader a new _____

Similes and Metaphors

_____ between two _____ things

A **simile** uses *like* or *as*.	A **metaphor** directly compares the things.
 She shook like a leaf.	 He is a ray of sunshine.

The Eagle
by Alfred, Lord Tennyson

He clasps the crag with crooked hands;
Close to the sun in lonely lands,
Ringed with the azure world, he stands.

The wrinkled sea beneath him crawls;
He watches from his mountain walls,
And like a thunderbolt he falls.

Idioms

_____ that do not share the same _____ as the separate _____ in the _____

It's raining cats and dogs.

Dad asked Maya to be quiet while he was on the phone. Carter was intentionally bothering Maya. Mom told Maya to ignore Carter, or she would play right into his hands. I could hardly keep a straight face when four-year-old Maya looked at our six-year-old brother and very seriously said, "I believe you should act your age."

Personification

giving _____ characteristics

to _____ , _____ ,

or _____

The alarm clock started screaming
for attention on the nightstand.

Hyperbole

an _____ to emphasize

a _____

My little brother asked me
a million times to borrow my new game.

Please let me play your game. Please let me play your game. Please let me play your game. Please let me play your game. Please let me play your game. Please let me play your game. Please let me play your game. Please let me play your game. Please let me play your

No!

My Shadow (excerpt)
by Robert Louis Stevenson

I have a little shadow that goes
    in and out with me,
And what can be the use of him
    is more than I can see.
He is very, very like me
    from the heels up to the head;
And I see him jump before me,
    when I jump into my bed.

The funniest thing about him
    is the way he likes to grow—
Not at all like proper children,
    which is always very slow;
For he sometimes shoots up taller
    like an India-rubber ball,
And he sometimes gets so little
    that there's none of him at all.

When Jonathan was walking home, a stray cat followed him up the steps and sat quietly outside the door, watching him closely. Jonathan made a sandwich. The cat continued to stare at him. Jonathan sighed. "I know it's not a good idea to feed a stray cat," he said, "but you look so hungry! I can't sit here and eat without feeding you too!"

Jonathan put some turkey on a plate for the cat. As Jonathan watched, she ate every scrap of turkey in the blink of an eye. "Wow!" Jonathan said, "You must have been starving. I wonder how long it has been since someone fed you."

Alliteration

_____ the first

_____ sound in several words

- -

Peter Piper picked a peck of pickled peppers.

Onomatopoeia

the use of words that _____ like

their _____

- -

As the door creaked open, a sigh escaped my lips. I could hear the drip, drip, drip of water from inside.

A lady wore a hat to the town's parade.
It had a big, red flower perched on top.
I saw her somewhere later, drinking
  lemonade;
I guess she prefers it to plain pop.

She did look peculiar in her flowered
  looks;
I'd never ever seen anything like it
  before.
She also had a bag in which she
  brought big books.
She stood smiling in front of Mr. Martin's
  store.

Then, two days later, I saw her wear
  a sock.
I think it was pink with purple polka dots.
She looked a little funny, but it wasn't
  quite a shock.
I guess she likes to dress up and visit
  town a lot!

Birches (excerpt)
by Robert Frost

When I see birches bend to left and right
Across the lines of straighter darker trees,
I like to think some boy's been swinging
  them.
But swinging doesn't bend them down
  to stay.
Ice-storms do that. Often you must have
  seen them
Loaded with ice a sunny winter morning
After a rain. They click upon themselves
As the breeze rises, and turn
  many-colored
As the stir cracks and crazes their enamel.

Using Word Relationships

Introduction

Review synonyms, antonyms, and multiple-meaning words. Write several words on the board such as *happy, sad, scared, hungry,* and *messy.* Have students think of synonyms and antonyms for each word. Encourage students to use vivid words. Record the suggestions for each word. Then, write two sentences on the board using a multiple-meaning word differently such as *Judd's chore was dusting the bookcase* and *There was a light dusting of snow on the ground.* Have students discuss how they knew the intended meaning of the word *dusting* in each sentence.

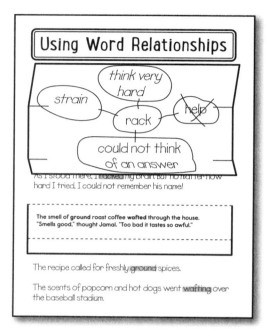

Creating the Notebook Page

Guide students through the following steps to complete the right-hand page in their notebooks.

1. Add a Table of Contents entry for the Using Word Relationships pages.

2. Cut out the title and glue it to the top of the page.

3. Discuss the types of word relationships that can help readers understand new words such as synonyms, antonyms, context clues, multiple-meaning words, etc. Below the title, list the types of word relationships readers can use to determine the meaning of unfamiliar words.

4. Cut out the trifolds. Fold both trifolds on the dashed lines so that the text and gray glue sections are on the outside of each piece. Apply glue to the gray glue sections and attach the pieces to the page. Place the piece with *rack* below the title.

5. Read the top passage. Look at the bold word. Open the flap and write the bold word in the center of the piece. Then, create a word web to use familiar words to give meaning to the bold word. For example, write synonyms, antonyms, context clues, other meanings that are not correct, non-examples, etc. (One student's word web will not look like another's.)

6. Write a sentence using the word below the trifold.

7. Repeat steps 5 and 6 with the bottom trifold. Use both words to create two separate word webs inside the piece. Write two sentences.

Reflect on Learning

To complete the left-hand page, have students describe in their own words how they can use word relationships as a strategy for defining unknown words while reading.

Using Word Relationships

The test was nearly over. Kyle was trying to **rack** his brain for an answer to the second question. He just could not come up with one.

glue

The smell of **ground** roast coffee **wafted** through the house. "Smells good," thought Jamal. "Too bad it tastes so awful."

glue

Tabs

Cut out each tab and label it. Apply glue to the back of each tab and align it on the outside edge of the page with only the label section showing beyond the edge. Then, fold each tab to seal the page inside.

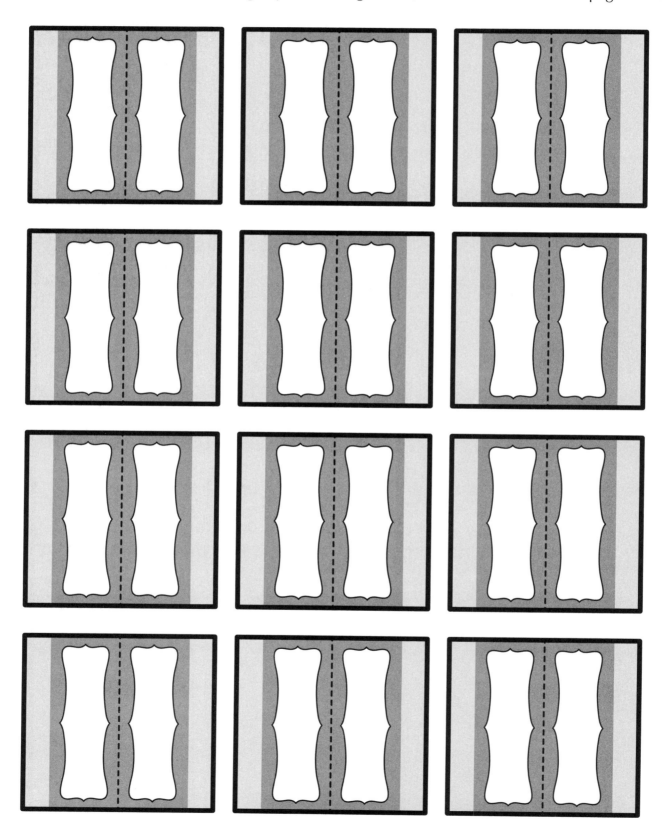

Cut out the KWL chart and cut on the solid lines to create three separate flaps. Apply glue to the back of the Topic section to attach the chart to a notebook page.

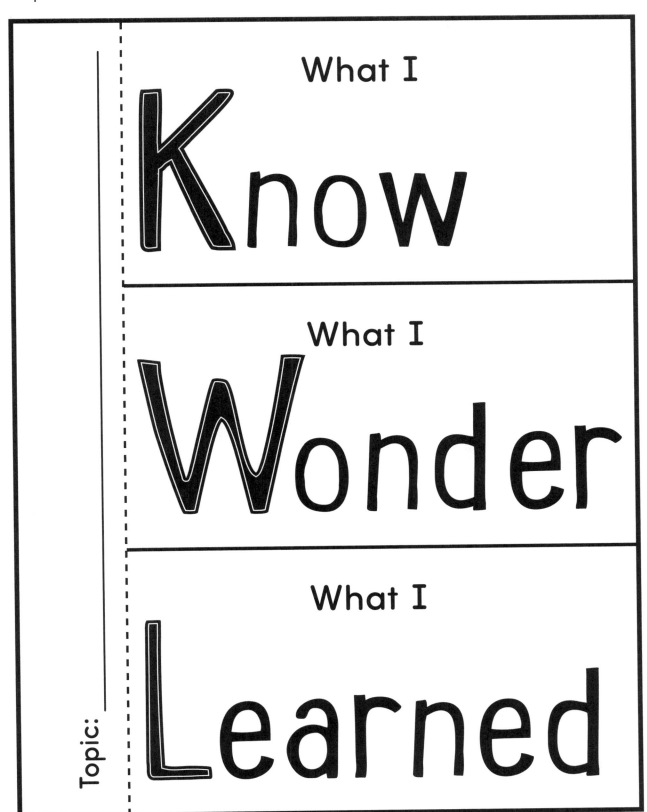

What I

Know

What I

Wonder

What I

Learned

Topic: _____

Library Pocket

Cut out the library pocket on the solid lines. Fold in the side tabs and apply glue to them before folding up the front of the pocket. Apply glue to the back of the pocket to attach it to a notebook page.

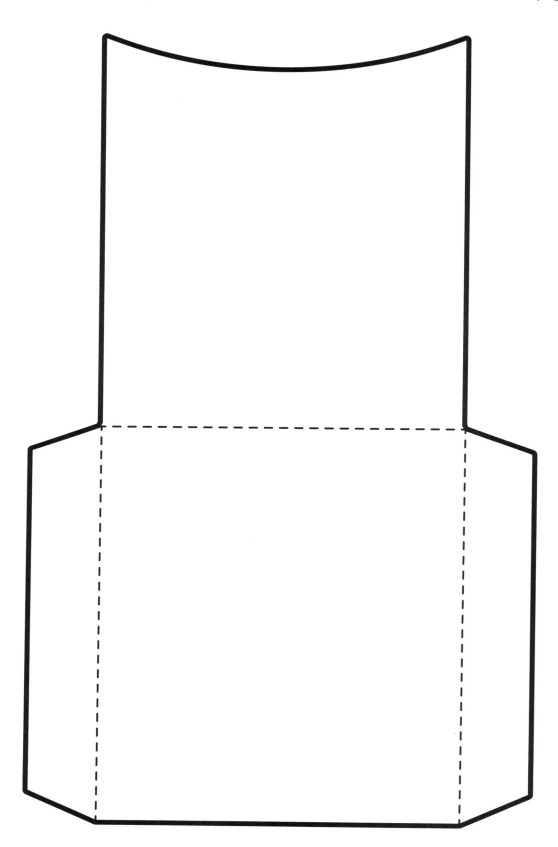

Envelope

Cut out the envelope on the solid lines. Fold in the side tabs and apply glue to them before folding up the rectangular front of the envelope. Fold down the triangular flap to close the envelope. Apply glue to the back of the envelope to attach it to a notebook page.

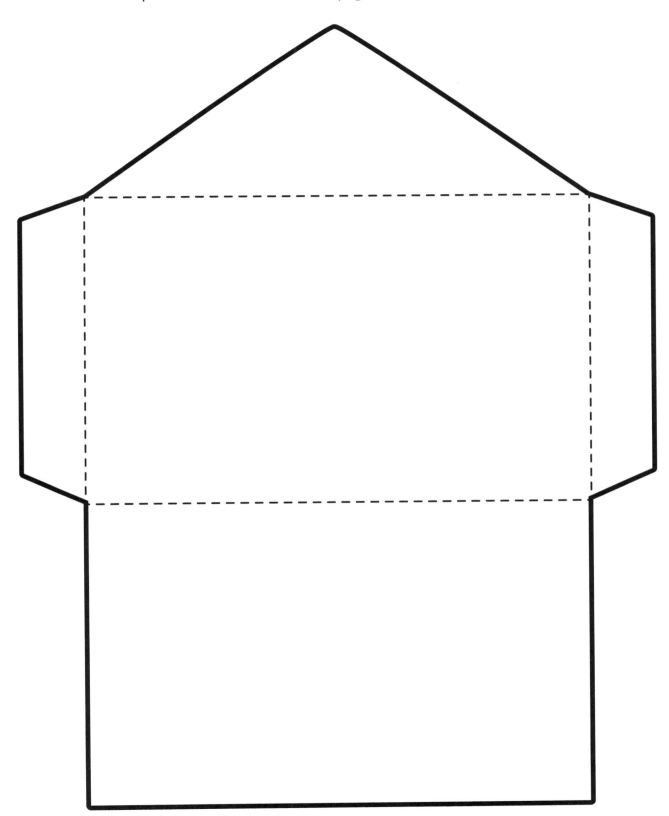

Pocket and Cards

Cut out the pocket on the solid lines. Fold over the front of the pocket. Then, apply glue to the tabs and fold them around the back of the pocket. Apply glue to the back of the pocket to attach it to a notebook page. Cut out the cards and store them in the envelope.

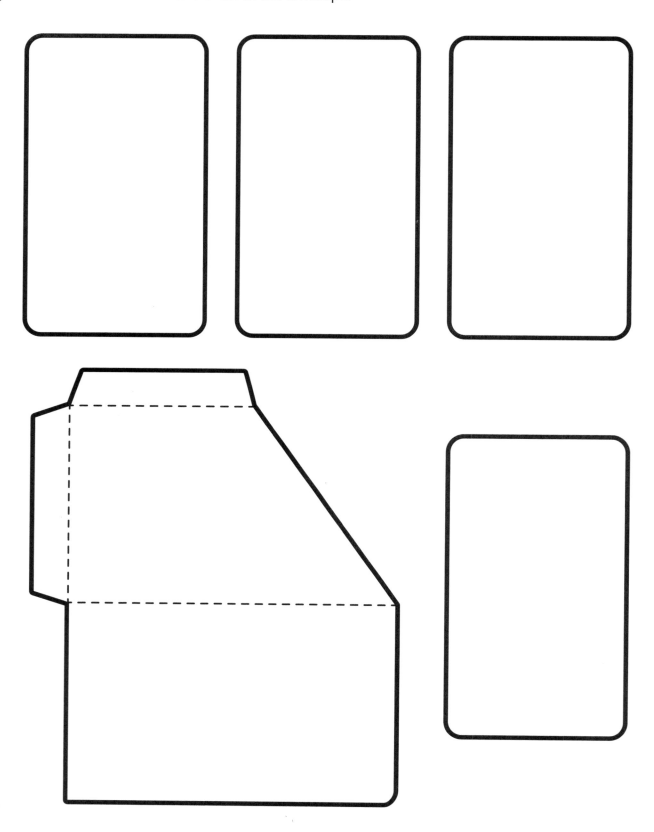

Six-Flap Shutter Fold

Cut out the shutter fold around the outside border. Then, cut on the solid lines to create six flaps. Fold the flaps toward the center. Apply glue to the back of the shutter fold to attach it to a notebook page.

If desired, this template can be modified to create a four-flap shutter fold by cutting off the bottom row. You can also create two three-flap books by cutting it in half down the center line.

Eight-Flap Shutter Fold

Cut out the shutter fold around the outside border. Then, cut on the solid lines to create eight flaps. Fold the flaps toward the center. Apply glue to the back of the shutter fold to attach it to a notebook page.

If desired, this template can be modified to create two four-flap shutter folds by cutting off the bottom two rows. You can also create two four-flap books by cutting it in half down the center line.

Flap Book—Eight Flaps

Cut out the flap book around the outside border. Then, cut on the solid lines to create eight flaps. Apply glue to the back of the center section to attach it to a notebook page.

If desired, this template can be modified to create a six-flap or two four-flap books by cutting off the bottom row or two. You can also create a tall four-flap book by cutting off the flaps on the left side.

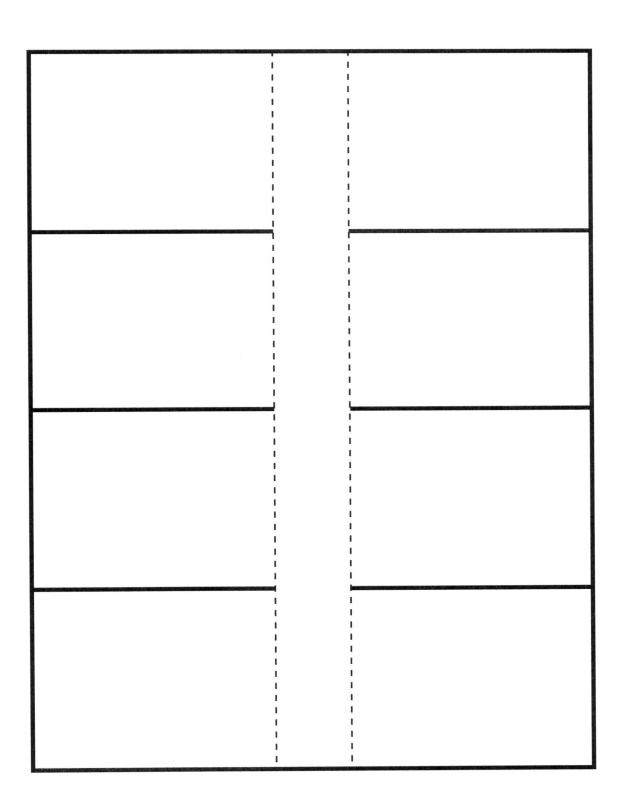

Flap Book—Twelve Flaps

Cut out the flap book around the outside border. Then, cut on the solid lines to create 12 flaps. Apply glue to the back of the center section to attach it to a notebook page.

If desired, this template can be modified to create smaller flap books by cutting off any number of rows from the bottom. You can also create a tall flap book by cutting off the flaps on the left side.

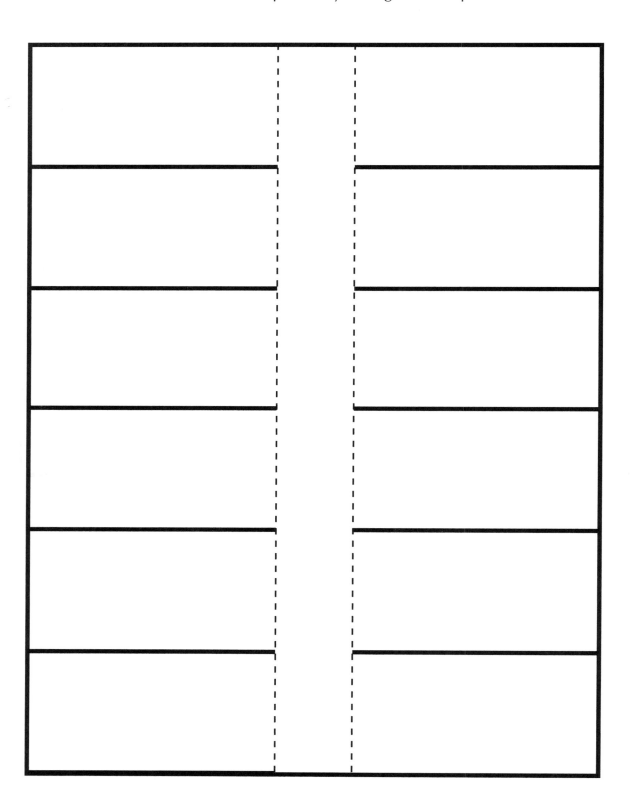

Shaped Flaps

Cut out each shaped flap. Apply glue to the back of the narrow section to attach it to a notebook page.

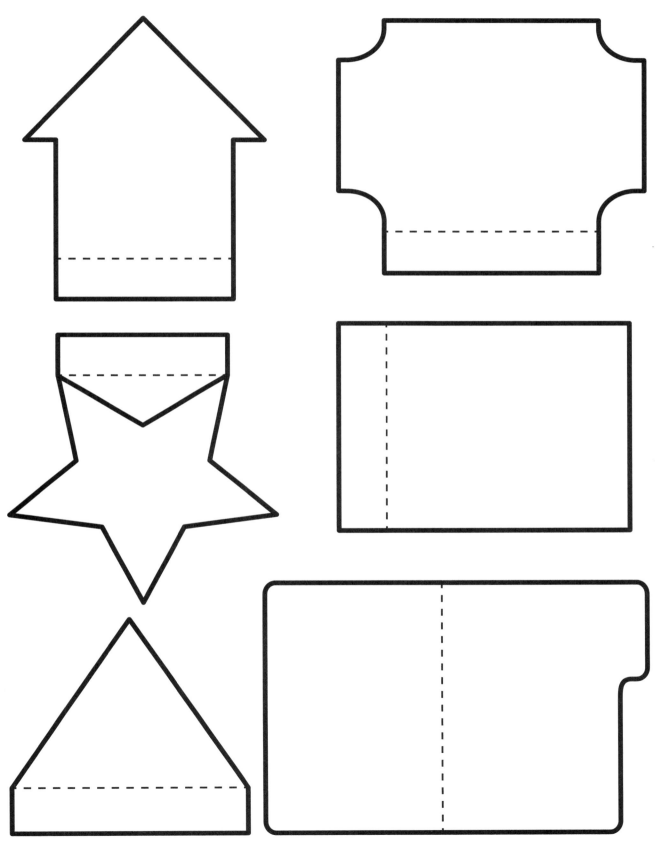

Shaped Flaps

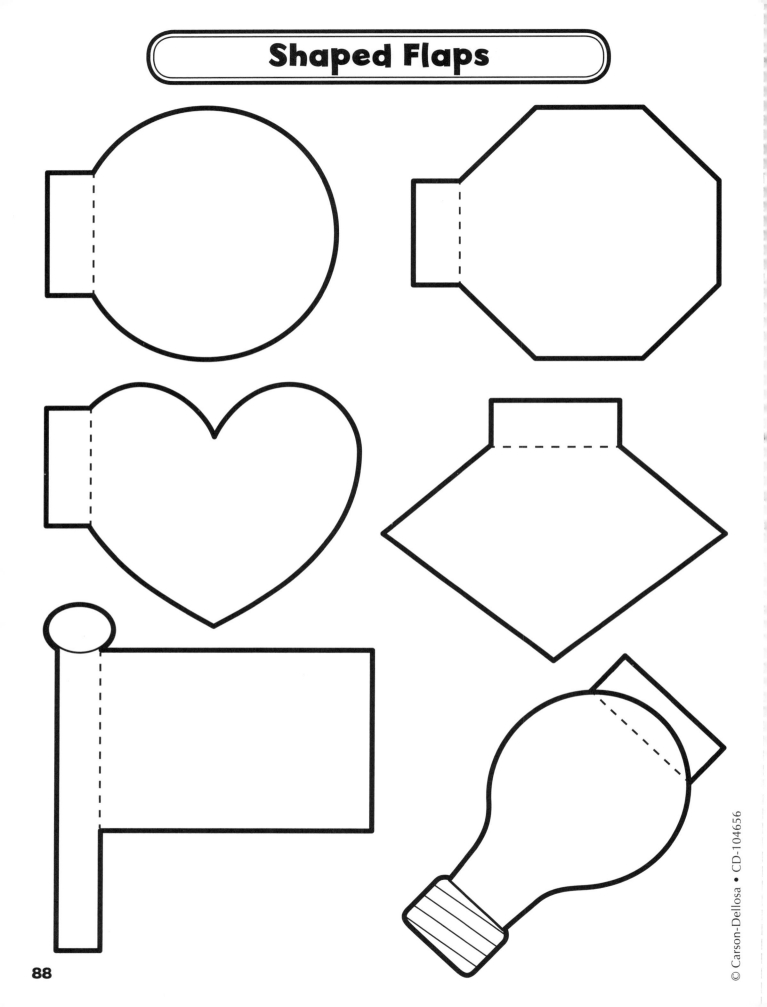

Interlocking Booklet

Cut out the booklet on the solid lines, including the short vertical lines on the top and bottom flaps. Then, fold the top and bottom flaps toward the center, interlocking them using the small vertical cuts. Apply glue to the back of the center panel to attach it to a notebook page.

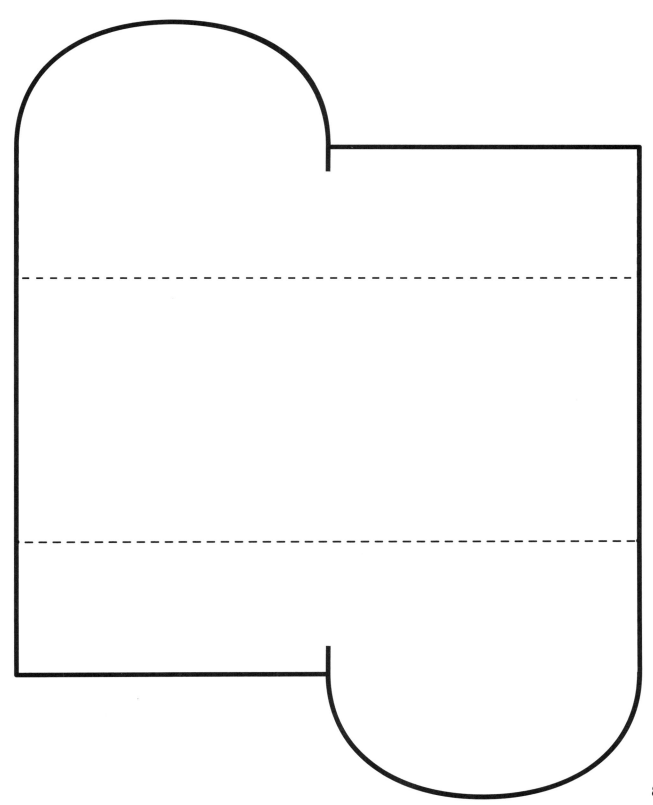

Four-Flap Petal Fold

Cut out the shape on the solid lines. Then, fold the flaps toward the center. Apply glue to the back of the center panel to attach it to a notebook page.

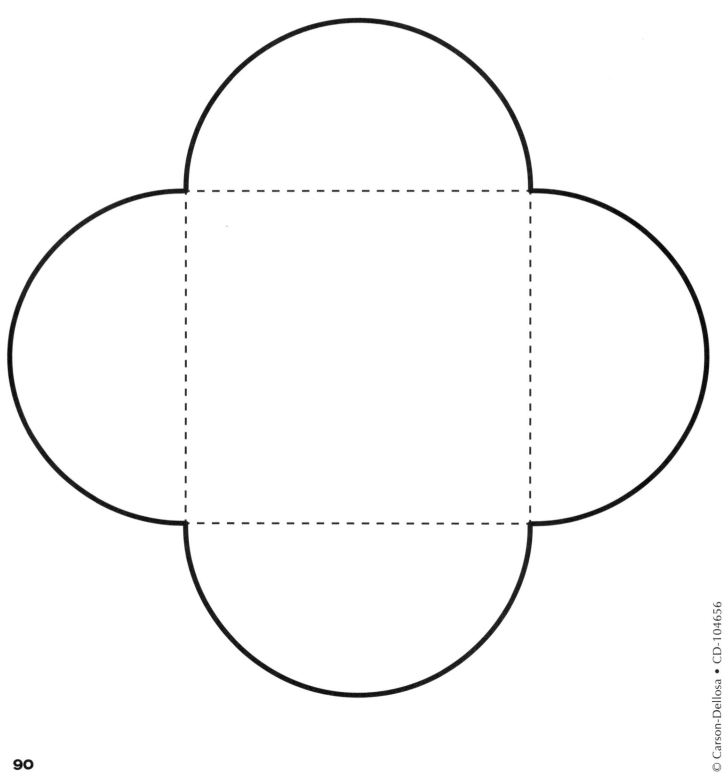

Six-Flap Petal Fold

Cut out the shape on the solid lines. Then, fold the flaps toward the center and back out. Apply glue to the back of the center panel to attach it to a notebook page.

Accordion Folds

Cut out the accordion pieces on the solid lines. Fold on the dashed lines, alternating the fold direction. Apply glue to the back of the last section to attach it to a notebook page.

You may modify the accordion books to have more or fewer pages by cutting off extra pages or by having students glue the first and last panels of two accordion books together.

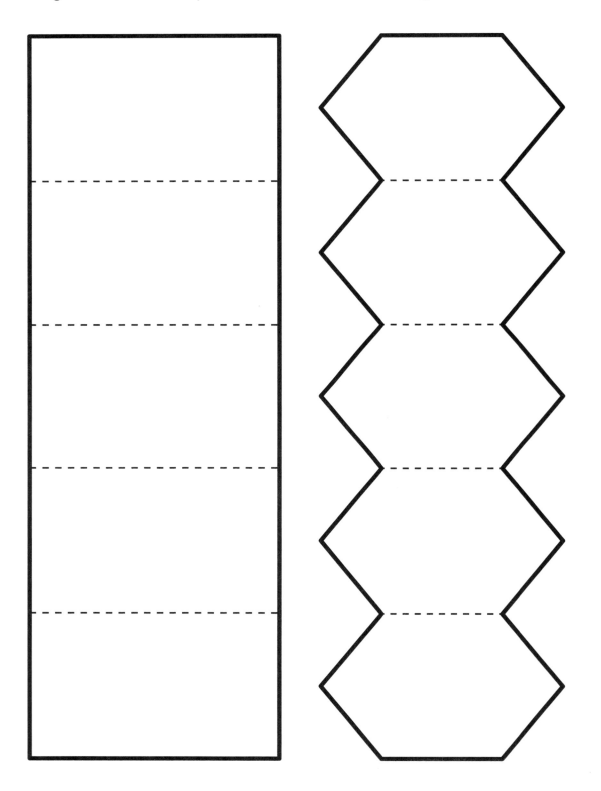

Accordion Folds

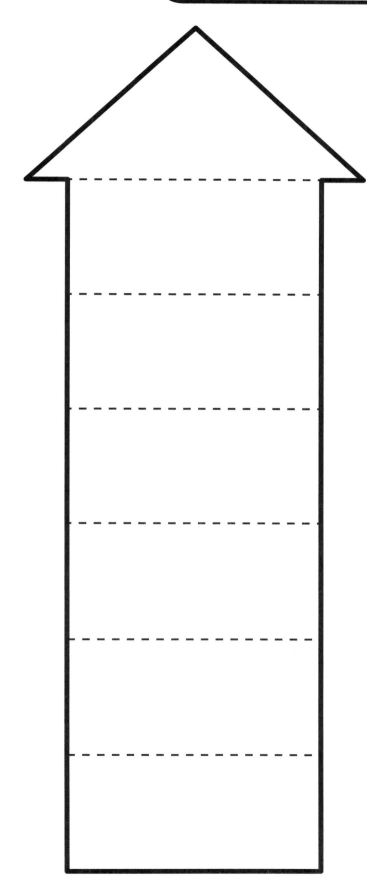

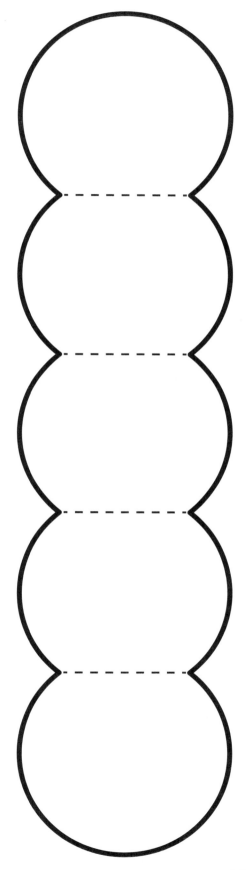

Clamshell Fold

Cut out the clamshell fold on the solid lines. Fold and unfold the piece on the three dashed lines. With the piece oriented so that the folds form an X with a horizontal line through it, pull the left and right sides together at the fold line. Then, keeping the sides touching, bring the top edge down to meet the bottom edge. You should be left with a triangular shape that unfolds into a square. Apply glue to the back of the triangle to attach the clamshell to a notebook page.

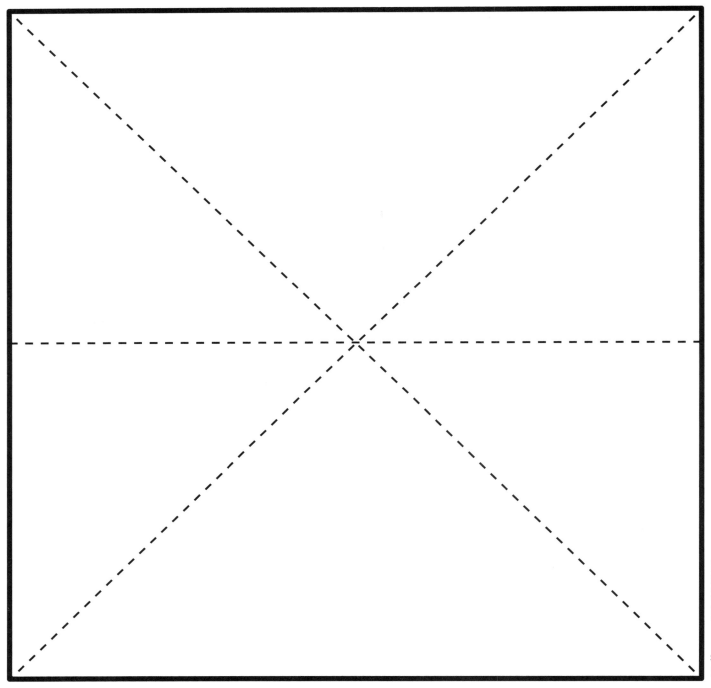

Puzzle Pieces

Cut out each puzzle along the solid lines to create a three- or four-piece puzzle. Apply glue to the back of each puzzle piece to attach it to a notebook page. Alternately, apply glue only to one edge of each piece to create flaps.

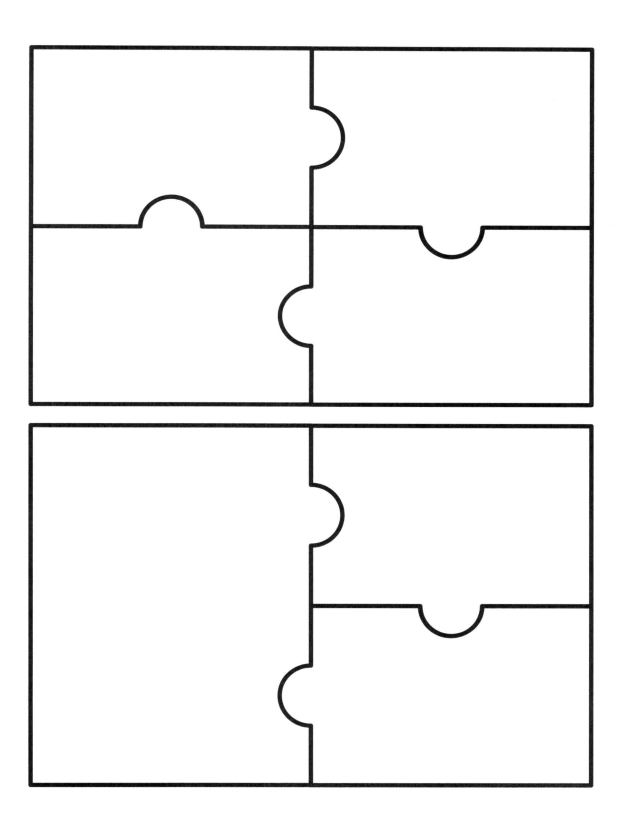

Flip Book

Cut out the two rectangular pieces on the solid lines. Fold each rectangle on the dashed lines. Fold the piece with the gray glue section so that it is inside the fold. Apply glue to the gray glue section and place the other folded rectangle on top so that the folds are nested and create a book with four cascading flaps. Make sure that the inside pages are facing up so that the edges of both pages are visible. Apply glue to the back of the book to attach it to a notebook page.

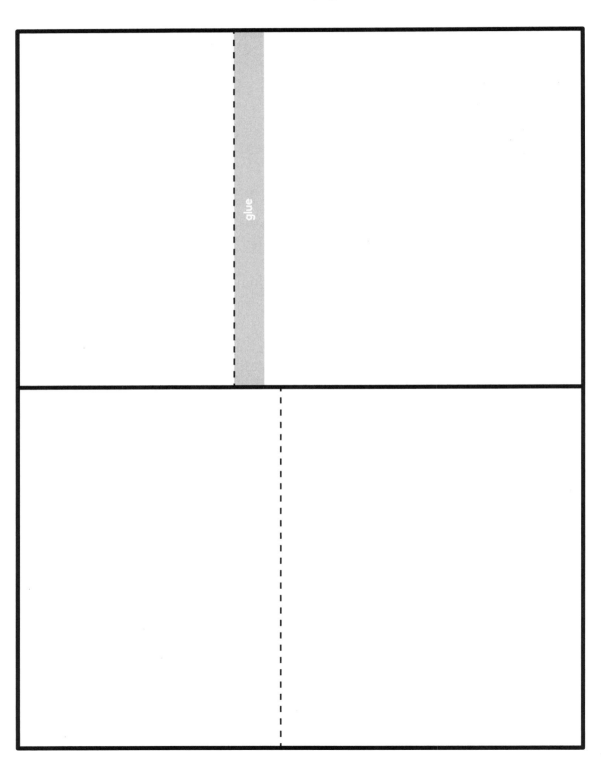

glue